TOWARD A PHENOMENOLOGY
OF EDUCATION

BOOKS BY J. GORDON CHAMBERLIN
PUBLISHED BY THE WESTMINSTER PRESS

Toward a Phenomenology of Education

*Freedom and Faith: New Approaches
to Christian Education*

Churches and the Campus

*Parents and Religion: A Preface
to Christian Education*

Toward a Phenomenology
of Education

by J. Gordon Chamberlin

The Westminster Press
Philadelphia

PUBLISHED BY THE WESTMINSTER PRESS®
PHILADELPHIA, PENNSYLVANIA

PRINTED IN THE UNITED STATES OF AMERICA

To Mark, Philip, Judith, Stephen
and all my students:
You have been my teachers

PREFACE

EDUCATION is always an activity, and each educational activity implies an educational theory. Understanding the theory is essential in order to understand the activity, yet most "educators," deeply involved in the practice of education, would be hard pressed to identify the basic theories which their practice expresses. The relation of theory and action is very complex, for action influences theory as often as theory guides action.

All of us become involved in the activities of education long before we have occasion, self-consciously, to reflect on assumptions lying behind our actions. When a person moves from conducting educational programs to teaching "education" courses he is pressed to look at the field from a new perspective. This has been my experience.

Students' questions and my desire to help them prepare for their educational responsibilities brought greater pressure on me than did "the developments in the field." But a self-conscious effort to find a more illuminating way to look at education exposes a person to the wide variety of possible perspectives. One should meet with skepticism the claim that a philosopher's view of education is more valid than an economist's, a psychologist's than a theologian's, or a sociologist's than a historian's. Nevertheless, the perspective we adopt tends to determine the categories established, the terminology employed, and finally what is seen. Thus the adequacy of a view of the field depends upon the inclusiveness of the perspective.

While attempting to reexamine the nature of education, during a sabbatical leave in Latin America, I was introduced to several writers on phenomenology and education. Their work suggested a distinctive view that would be broad and inclusive and would focus attention upon the essential character of the social phenomenon—education.

This study is an attempt to explore the assumption that education can be viewed as a whole and that the necessary elements of the phenomenon revealed in the process will provide fresh illumination into both educational activity and theory for anyone—teacher, student, parent, board member, administrator, and even professor—who tries to understand the nature of the enterprise called "education."

Special appreciation is due Prof. Edward A. Farley, with whom I have discussed many aspects of this study, though the way our discussions have been incorporated—as they have been at various points—reflects my interpretation. Acknowledging his helpfulness does not imply that he agrees with or is to be held responsible for the results.

And thanks is due Mrs. Elizabeth Eakin for typing the manuscript.

J. G. C.

Pittsburgh, Pennsylvania

CONTENTS

INTRODUCTION

EDUCATION is a vast social phenomenon of the twentieth century. Every educational statistic is immense: the hordes of students in schools and universities; the armies of teachers and administrators; the flood of textbooks and books about education; the proliferation of types of educational enterprises; the continually expanding bureaucracies; the enormous budgets; *and* the remaining illiteracy; the need for more teachers; the population explosion; the new skills required by the technological revolution; the unsolved problems of resources and methodologies; the confusion about philosophy.

Education is a huge umbrella. So many ideas, institutions, and activities crowd under the shade of the term that the word "education" is virtually meaningless. What is the quality of education in this country? The answer depends upon what is meant by education. How much education is provided by this city? The answer depends upon what is meant by education. How can I get an education? That depends upon what you mean by education.

For many people education refers to what is done in schools. Understanding the extent and complexity of education in this context requires a comprehension of the tremendous variety of institutions of learning and the organizations that they require. Within the schools are found the remains of many different ideas about education expressed in patterns of organization, methods of teaching, and physical arrangements of classrooms, as well as in explicitly formulated philosophies of education. The different philosophies of education are not products of the educational field alone; they grow from the total social situation in which the schools are located. And since the social context of schools in various cultures is so different that "school" can mean many different things, the term is an inadequate synonym for education.

For many people education refers to teaching, and "teaching" most frequently connotes transmission of ideas or patterns of behavior from teacher to pupil. Yet each philosophy of education implies its own idea of what good teaching is, and the devotees of each philosophy attempt to develop a process that incorporates the distinctive emphasis of their position. But the step from theory to practice is a very difficult one, in part because of the great variety of teachers whose personalities profoundly influence their ways of teaching. Students in schools of education are frequently amused (sometimes disillusioned) by this difficulty when they discover discrepancies between the theory of education propounded by their teachers and the patterns of education practiced by those same teachers, which documents in a vivid way the problem with the word "teaching" in expressing the meaning of education.

For many people "education" is synonymous with "learning," and is expressed particularly in the idea that a person can be "self-educated." While many educators seem to assume that the way people learn can be identified in some one basic process, there is little agreement among educators on whether that process is trial and error, stimulus-response, problem-solving, or intuition. Each theory of learning suggests its own distinctive idea of teaching and of the educational processes which would contribute to learning. In reality school systems often include different theories of learning, and therefore attempt to fit together processes based on conflicting assumptions. When attention is shifted from how a person learns to what is to be learned, it is obvious that most of this learning is acquired at other times and in other places than schools or formal education. Thus "learning" is too inclusive a concept to provide discrimination in use of educational terms and meanings.

The confusion that comes in the use of these terms is a reflection of the pluralism in the field. Education is such a vast enterprise all over the world that there is a natural reluctance to attempt a totally inclusive view. Yet whether educators realize it or not every activity in which they engage is derivative from a greater movement, a worldwide reality. Education in one country cannot be understood in isolation from education in another country, for today it is an international activity. Each year sees a heavier international commerce in educational ideas and practices, both present and past. To understand the field, one must look at the total phenomenon.

This book was written while engaged, for several months during a sabbatical, in a study of an educational institution in Argentina.[1] The direct encounter with the problems and perspectives of education in a culture quite different from that of one's homeland is part of the experience of more and more educators and students in this century. The experience of relationships and differences in views of education makes the need of a wider perspective a personal one. The generality of the use of the word "education" itself, in spite of its many meanings, may indicate an implicit unity or relationship behind the diversity which deserves careful reexamination. How is it possible to think of education so that the deeper interrelationship may be formative in developing one's own philosophy?

One of the handicaps in seeking an answer to that question is the common assumption that education is a normative discipline. Most writing in the field is admonitory, telling administrators and teachers what they ought to do, attacking schools for their failures, pleading for special causes, trying to influence legislation, or giving advice to parents. This may be a salutary evidence of passionate concern (whatever the motive) about education, but much of the concern is misdirected because of its limited perspective. The normative approach tends to decide too early what is or is not "education" and also tends to make value judgments before all relevant factors have been considered.[2] This suggests that a descriptive approach to education may provide easier access to the immense variety of factors that ought to be considered.

The question What is education? is being raised with new urgency in recent years, both because of the confusion of concepts in the field, and because education is deriving benefits from the expanding interest in linguistic analysis. One approach to the question has been by way of asking whether education is a "discipline." This consideration was spurred by a collection of papers that appeared in *The Discipline of Education*.[3] The writers were about equally divided between those who felt education was or was not a discipline, but this disagreement generally reflected a prior disagreement about what constitutes a discipline. More recently Marc Belth has addressed the issue very helpfully in *Education as a Discipline*,[4] contending that the discipline of education is "the study of models of thinking." By attempting to identify the "root" of the concept of education, Belth has so narrowed the term that he is really speaking of "the study of education" rather than the broader, more inclusive activity of conducting educational programs.

Analytic philosophy has made extensive inroads into the field of educational philosophy during the past decade. Significant pioneering work has been done by R. S. Peters in England and Israel Scheffler in the United States.[5] Surely clarity and precision in the use of language, images, concepts, and metaphors throughout the broad spectrum of educational activities are of crucial importance. It may be difficult for the ardent protagonists for the analytic approach, however, to identify some of the limitations and inadequacies of such an approach.

The analytic examination of educational concepts needs to

be balanced by an equally careful examination of the processes and institutions which are always involved in an educational activity. When teachers or students or philosophers
argue about the meaning of words, they are already involved
in a social process which is more than a conception, and which
is part of the context that may sharply influence the meaning
of the concepts.

A distinction needs to be made between "education" and
"the study of education." Each may employ a variety of disciplines, and each requires disciplined thinking, but for either
one to be a discipline would require the identification of some
specific element, as Belth has done, as the object of study.
When that is agreed upon by the professionals in the field then
there can be constructive debate about the appropriate methodologies for studying that object, and if such methodologies
are generally accepted it will be possible to designate this as
a discipline.

Without attempting at this point to enter the debate as to
whether education is a discipline, or even to make a judgment
upon the validity of such an inquiry as a way to understand
what education is, the contention of this book is that the distinctiveness of education (i.e., conducting educational activities, whatever the object of study) cannot be reduced to a particular element; there is no single key to the nature of education. Because the field is so vast, the effort to understand it
must begin with the comprehensive, inclusive view that attempts to deal honestly with its worldwide complexity and
diversity rather than to simplify it in advance by premature
specificity.[6] In this field a wide-angle lens is imperative. The
assumption with which such an exploration must begin is that
education is some kind of a set of interrelated factors. Clearly
this "set" is always an observable *social* phenomenon (even in
its simplest form it involves teacher and learner) so it can
yield to a phenomenological analysis of its reality.

"Phenomenology" may be as difficult to identify as "education." Professor Kockelmans has edited a 555-page book[7] de-

voted to "the answering of one vital question: What is phenomenology?" [8] However, the term refers to a philosophical
movement whose most influential figure was the German philosopher, Edmund Husserl. Among other distinguished philosophers sharing in the development of the movement are Martin Heidegger, Maurice Merleau-Ponty, and Paul Ricoeur.[9]

This philosophical movement is identified by a distinctive
methodology. One description of this methodology is given
by Martin Heidegger:

> The expression "phenomenology" signifies primarily a
> *methodological conception*. This expression does not
> characterize the what of the objects of philosophical re-
> search as subject-matter, but rather the *how* of that
> research. The more genuinely a methodological concept
> is worked out and the more comprehensively it deter-
> mines the principles on which a science is to be con-
> ducted, all the more primordially is it rooted in the way
> we come to terms with the things themselves. . . . Thus
> the term "phenomenology" expresses a maxim which can
> be formulated as "to the things themselves." It is opposed
> to all free-floating constructions and accidental findings;
> it is opposed to taking over any conceptions which only
> seem to have been demonstrated; it is opposed to those
> pseudo-questions which parade themselves as "prob-
> lems," often for generations at a time. Yet this maxim,
> one may rejoin, is abundantly self-evident, and it ex-
> presses, moreover, the underlying principle of any scien-
> tific knowledge whatsoever.[10]

Phenomenological analysis has been employed in the study
of many aspects of human existence.[11] However, it has not
been used in the study of education except for a few writers
in Germany and South America. The most serious effort was
made forty years ago when Ernst Kreick, a German peda-
gogue, used the Husserlian methodology in a book *Grundriss
der Erziehungs-wissenschaft*[12] in trying to develop "a pure
science of education."

Perhaps a new look at education, employing some of the
tools of phenomenological analysis, will contribute to a deeper

understanding of the essential nature of the vast field. The pattern of study employed here "parallels" the modes of critical phenomenological analysis adapted to the character of the phenomenon being examined. The methodology employed here will not follow Kreick in attempting to develop a pure science of education, for to do so would be to assume that the field can be "a pure science" before analyzing it. Nor is this an attempt to identify education with the problems of consciousness (as in Husserl) or with Being (as in Heidegger). The open stance with which this study begins is more culturally than existentially orientated. A vast and diverse phenomenon called "education" is observable in every culture. The analysis and description to be made here will not attempt to reduce the concepts of one culture to those of another, nor to make a comparative study as though translation from one culture to another would be simply made.[13] It will, however, attempt to consider the total phenomenon in order to discover its necessary elements and suggest an order of their relationship.

Some branches of phenomenology have consciously eliminated "norms" from consideration,[14] not because they are irrelevant but because the phenomenon can be analyzed on its own terms without applying a priori norms. The result, of course, is only as valid as the inclusiveness of the range of phenomena taken into account. Though education should not be thought of as mainly a normative discipline, still norms are involved in education and it would not be possible to analyze the whole field without considering these norms, both as they are expressed in philosophies of education and as they are incorporated into educational programs.

Belth began his study with the question—Is education a discipline?—and thus was led by logical steps to move from identifying the nature of disciplines to stipulating the nature of education. There is an element of such circular thinking in any effort to identify and describe a field. The present study has started with a different question in order to hold off as long as possible from arriving at a definition, though it is obvious that the process of selecting phenomena to include in the broad category of "educational activities" implies some operational definition, otherwise all educational phenomena would have to be included, and that would be impossible. It is recognized, of course, that no matter how neutral or objective one may try to be every person brings extrinsic standards into the process of selection, choice, and description. In other words, any observer of education views the phenomenon from the perspective of his own world view, his own *optique*. His basic philosophic stance will show through sooner or later. This point the phenomenologist admits, yet he believes that because he is particularly aware of the problem he can set aside or hold in abeyance his prior commitments in order that the process of description may be as neutral as possible.

Part of the phenomenon of education is the activity of articulating philosophies of education. These, too, may be subjected to a phenomenological analysis, and such a study may contribute to the field by identifying the elements that are essential to an adequate philosophy of education.

What follows is presented more as a prolegomenon than as a philosophy of education. It suggests a somewhat different way of viewing[15] the variegated social activities referred to as "education," and a way to describe them which indicates their nature and interrelationships. Description cannot solve all the problems of education,[16] but hopefully it contributes to their clarification, sharpening the focus upon issues by viewing them from new perspectives.

Eight chapters are devoted to viewing education from new perspectives. Chapter IX suggests a possible definition of "education" in the light of the analysis. The references, quotations, and comments that follow indicate some of the major writers and summarize some of the major works dealing with many of the issues arising in the analysis, as well as offering quotations which I have found to be illuminating for my own thinking.

The field of education includes such diverse traditions, institutions, and theories that the first problem for anyone who seeks to study the whole field is "where to begin?" Since every concept of education includes learning—though not every idea of education includes teachers or institutions—this would suggest that the most comprehensive view of education begins with learning.

Since there are many learning theories, any effort to start with a definition of "learning" would automatically narrow the scope of the field to be examined. An approach that begins with description rather than definition can provide a more comprehensive first step. It is here that we will begin.

As is apparent from the contents, the first chapter will not approach the examination of learning as a psychological discipline, tracing the functions of the brain, examining synapses and neurograms. Much significant work has been done in laboratory, hospital, and classroom during the past generation in such studies of human mental activities. Similarly, over a longer period of time, philosophers have made significant contributions to the understanding of how knowledge is acquired, arranged, and used. The value of such psychological and philosophical studies is not to be questioned, unless someone asserts that he has the only valid approach to the understanding of learning.

The analysis that follows begins with the obvious social phenomenon that human beings can, and are expected to, learn—whatever one means by that word. What we discover if we have the patience to examine in some detail the vast ranges of learning which society expects of each individual may provide a larger frame of reference for the psychological studies. It may also provide a new perspective upon the distinctive philosophical question about what is important to know.

Chapter I

LEARNING

LEARNING is both a natural capacity and a societal necessity for every person. Society weaves a web of expectations around each individual and attempts to guide what he will become and when and how. Some of these expectations are explicit, particularly later in life, but most of them are implicit. They are discovered when a person breaks unwritten rules.

Societal expectations are expressed through many agencies —the tribe, the family, intimate social groups, occupational structures, political entities of city, state, or nation. In simple, closed, and static societies these expectations may constitute a comprehensive interrelated system. However, there are now very few such isolated societies. The overwhelming majority of the people of the world are increasingly exposed to different patterns of thought, belief, and behavior. There is no way for a society, even the most withdrawn or controlled, to escape completely the dynamic pressures of contemporary history. Open societies, to whatever degree they are open, cannot integrate what is expected of individuals, so each person is exposed to the resulting diversity of expectations about what is to be learned.

The catalog of what a baby born today will be expected to learn in the next three score and ten years is beyond our reckoning. However, it is possible to identify the *ranges of learning* to which he will be exposed and among which he will be expected to make some appropriation.

The typology of ranges of learning that follows is descriptive and indicative rather than normative or exhaustive. It is ordered primarily around the sequence in which a child meets the various types of things he must learn in order to be a normal member of his society. Each range of learning includes many facets of distinctive content; each tends to rely on particular capacities; each may be aided by certain types of setting; and each may imply particular conducive processes for both teaching and learning.

The categories developed here are intended only as a means for discerning the various types of reality that are encountered in learning. They are somewhat arbitrary, for reality cannot be split into unrelated parts. Every culture incorporates its own interpretation of the interrelationship among all ranges, just as they are related within the learner as he interprets their meaning for his existence.

The following is a brief analysis of ten ranges of learning in terms of content, capacities, setting and processes:

BODILY DEVELOPMENT

Content. To live means, at the least, to maintain minimal bodily health. While the definition of health varies greatly from society to society, early in life each child is expected to learn to care for his body. Physical growth under normal circumstances is natural, and the learning expected is usually directed toward giving freedom to that growth. In many primitive tribes, of course, there have been traditions of distortion of early growth, such as foot-binding or disfigurement. Whether the early teaching about bodily care is consciously handled in the home or is only implied in the general patterns of home life, every society develops standards of physical conduct and care which all children are expected to learn, such as patterns of elimination, of cleanliness, of safety in traffic, how to swim, how to handle injuries or prevent them, and group responsibility for exercise.

Later as children are brought into formally organized school settings, concern for bodily care is institutionalized. The setup of the school program may attempt to make movement to and from the building safe for the children, or it may provide clean rooms, convenient toilets, lighted stairs, and ventilation. Curricula include classroom teaching about the body and its care in hygiene, in biology or home economics courses, or in programs on school conduct. In some circumstances schools have initiated programs showing children how to brush their teeth, wash their hands, and encouraging better dietary practices at home. The school's concern for bodily development is also expressed in play periods, athletics, sports events, and physical education classes.

When a person moves from school into adult social responsibility other kinds of bodily development are usually demanded. Many occupations require special physical capacities and dexterity. Airplane pilots need better vision than farmers, carpenters develop muscles that atrophy for stenographers, and ice skaters need a sense of balance and rhythm. Athletes, surgeons, miners, have to spend years in cultivation of particular physical attributes.

Meanwhile, all adults have to learn about the changes of bodily care brought about by aging. Physical handicaps bring special problems, both of learning how to adjust to the handicap and also how to accept it if it threatens normal activity or social acceptance. Women are confronted by the need to learn new things about bodily development as they go through childbearing years, and later the menopausal period. Each man is faced by the need to adjust his "physical output" to his own physical capacity, as he faces the period of physical decline. Maintaining health may become such a preoccupation of the society that social agencies are forced to initiate concerted programs of reeducation for their clients.

Different sectors of society express these social expectations in different ways. Etiquette expresses certain kinds of physical expectation, as well as social customs, within the family and intimate groups. Views of health may differ widely but every society needs a healthy population to conduct its work or to fight its battles. As a society changes technologically its expectations of bodily development for work will change accordingly. A farmer, for instance, uses different physical capacities when he is weeding a cornfield with a hoe than when he is operating a complex power machine to kill weeds with new chemicals.

One of the ways which adults attempt to maintain health is by recreation. While recreation in urban culture may be mostly for spectators there are still millions of fishermen, golfers, mountain climbers, ballplayers, skaters, hunters, and bowlers who look for the lore available to be learned from books, from magazines, or from the firsthand accounts of the experts. Each of these patterns of play requires the learning of particular physical abilities. While its forms may change from youth to age, recreation can become a major preoccupation particularly in the greater leisure time available in technically advanced societies.

Bodily development also involves the whole range of medical practice. From simple home remedies passed by word of mouth from generation to generation to the most advanced technical developments in relating physics to bodily ills, there are things to be learned. The concern for health has proliferated a vast array of medical agencies devoted to providing prevention and treatment of disease. From the general practitioner to the complex of a huge hospital, many services may not be understood by all patients, but the objective is that every person will learn enough about modern medicine so that he will know how to escape quacks, where to go for appropriate treatment, and have a general understanding of what specialists are doing. Many agencies, public and private, participate in attempting to provide public information for the continuing reeducation of all persons about medical matters.

Mental health is increasingly a concern of most societies, extensively incorporated into the programs of schools and universities, with clinics and therapists, special hospitals, and vast public education activities in newspapers, books, television, and radio all devoted to helping people to learn about their own psychic patterns of life and their implications for individual and group relationships.

Capacities. Basic to the whole range of bodily development are the capacities of coordination and discipline. Obviously every society hopes to develop concern on the part of each individual about the values of bodily care held by that society, but whatever the work in which an individual is engaged the dimensions of physical activity require coordination—writing, painting, speaking, walking, running, balancing balls, or standing, and each in turn requires some self-discipline—to brush one's teeth after each meal or every night, to bathe daily, weekly, or monthly, to drive on the left in England and on the right in the United States, or to balance on forty-story ledges while washing windows.

Beyond coordination and discipline, of course, must be a capacity to comprehend the reasons for health so that there may be sufficient motivation for consistent general care. When a society expects its members to maintain health without force it assumes the capacity to understand principles and relate principles to behavior. Mobile or changing societies also assume that their members are willing to accept new findings about the factors that aid or hinder good bodily development.

Settings. There is no one locus for learning about bodily development. Most aspects of this range are learned in the process of participating in home and community events, or in occupational training. Innumerable agencies have been set up to provide both occupational and recreational training. Schools, from kindergarten to university, usually incorporate physical exercise in their total programs. Enlightened industries may provide facilities for the physical welfare of workers in improved working conditions, in recreational areas and programs, and in establishing health requirements for executives.

The cultural and religious setting may have a direct effect upon what is to be learned about the body. Not only are there types of bodily skill expected of all members of some societies (for instance, the Eskimos), but sharply contrasting relative values are given to various aspects of bodily care, such as exposure, cleanliness, or longevity. In most parts of the world, however, the knowledge of medicine has encouraged good health as a value and the spread of health programs by official agencies of governments.

Processes. Each person's learning about bodily development is highly existential. He learns from within the physical attributes with which he is endowed. The person who is physically normal experiences directly all the phases of the life process, so that what society expects him to learn automatically involves him in reflection upon his own physical condition. The person with a handicap may allow his physical debility to color all the other ranges of learning, and may never be able to appreciate the general social expectations for learning about bodily development. Thus the process, from the learner's point of view, is one of inescapable adjustment to the physical condition of his life, both in endowment and in what has happened to the body during that lifetime.

The processes by which bodily control and discipline are learned are repetition, practice, and repeated testing. In school or in sports the testing may be an athletic contest, or during an appointment with the dentist, or while being examined at an Army induction center, or when applying for an insurance policy. These become the ways by which most people "learn" about their bodies and what may be required to maintain them in keeping with societal expectations. But the most common "test" is daily when strength or dexterity are pitted against the jobs to be done.

SYMBOL SYSTEMS

Content. A mother's look into the face of a newborn child is the first token of the symbol system he will be expected to learn and use throughout his lifetime. Facial expressions, bodily gestures, sounds, are employed with meaning and a child soon interprets that meaning in relation to his own wants and needs. He is the recipient of symbolic acts to which he must learn to respond. They may be such specific acts as patting, fondling, smiling, and cooing, or the more general parental acts such as feeding, washing, dressing, and providing for the infant. This is his first introduction to the ubiquitous range of verbal and nonverbal communication that marks humanity. Soon he will begin to learn the speech of his family and community, and only much later may he learn how the language is the carrier of the total culture into which he has been born. Language-learning will continue throughout life because the vocabulary of any language system is greater than any one person's knowledge, but also because language is continually changing. Symbolic acts, whether individual or social, include a vast range that must be learned and relearned whenever there is change in the acts and in their meaning. Symbolic acts may be patriotic, like saluting the flag, or religious, like praying, or economic, like the transfer of a check.

The symbol system to be learned also includes material objects that express the history of the particular people and provide items for its self-identity. These, too, may be either secular or religious symbols.

All these aspects of the symbol system of a culture may become the focus of self-conscious study in art, philosophy, or theology, yet the formal structures of these fields change when events alter meanings, so that different interpretations and different symbols emerge from those events.

"Systems" of symbolics may be distinguished in four types: *personal*—habitual or characteristic acts that project a particular personality; *social*—symbols that have a social origin and meaning; *material*—symbols that may be expressed in artifacts, including written language; and *actions*—speech, dance, facial and bodily expressions. All are learned and require relearning throughout life.

Capacities. Man is a symbol-constituted and symbol-creating creature.[17] Every individual has the capacity to respond to both symbolic acts and material. However, the content of meaning that is communicated requires interpretation on the part of the respondent. The capacity for such interpretation is relative to the emotional adjustment and intellectual ability of the person, and these are influenced both by his native endowment and by prior experience. Thus the response is of the whole person and is both conscious and unconscious.

Settings. Every setting in life—home, community, school, work, and recreation—is the locale for learning the symbol system of one's culture. The self-conscious study of symbolic expression—whether of one's own culture or of another—may be carried on in the home, in the school, or on the psychiatrist's couch.[18]

Processes. Symbolic acts are a form of communication in which both the actor and the respondent are engaged in trial and error testing of the meaning of the act. Learning the meaning of symbolic acts is a radically subjective activity in which the interpretation of meaning is always locked within the receiver and can be expressed only by further symbolic acts.

Language, as one mode of symbolic expression and communication, bears an objective "freight," for it comes to a particular person from his cultural history; yet this burden must be learned and its meaning is relative to many social and psychological factors in each person. The use of language bears the same double movement—a general community rootage with objective implications yet used relative to the meaning it has for the speaker or writer.[19]

Symbols. In learning to use language a person is, at the same time, being initiated into interpretation of the world. Language is a crystallization of the meaning of reality by those who have gone before, but it is also the tool by which a person shapes his understanding of reality. The exchange of words, phrases, and sentences, along with the emotional di-

mensions of their use, control the appearance and response a
person makes to his situation in the world. Through language
he meets and conditions his history, but is never able totally
to express or exhaust its meaning. Language is always an inadequate tool because our contact with reality is never limited
only to conscious expression. Language helps to sharpen and
focus perception, and though it may shape us, it is always
subject to creative use in new ways.

The learning of language, therefore, includes both the
principles and structure of the objective symbol system, and
the common usage with its particular meanings.

SOCIAL RELATIONSHIPS

Content. The birth of a human being immediately exposes
an infant, whether in a remote Eskimo settlement or in the
midst of a megalopolis, to a welter of social relationships.
Every society is made up of many groupings, small and large,
in which each person has to find his way. The more mobile a
people the greater the number of structures which each person
must learn about, finding his responsibilities and status in
each one. Every society develops a panorama of customs related to the basic events of life, and these must be learned
in terms of each grouping within the society.

Every person spends his entire life in this complex web of
social interaction. His group relationship is continually changing and all through life he is faced with learning what the
various groups hold as important, and how to relate to the
various levels of ingroup and outgroup prescribed ways.

Some of these relationships are *direct*. The primary and most
intimate group is the family, and beyond that the extended
family. Within these is a complex of relations to parents, siblings, kin, and in-laws. Usually a child is exposed to all of
these from the first day of life, so he must learn how he is
related to whom. Seldom can these relationships be standardized in a society because the particular relational patterns de-

pend upon the individuals involved and their own distinctive views of what that relationship should be.

Beyond the extended family—which itself can take a wide variety of forms—are secondary small groups or associations. Early in life these may be circles of playmates or teams or gangs, but these relationships may, in turn, be determined by broader relations to class or community or racial group. Usually children in a wealthy suburb do not go to school or play in the park with children from a public housing project. Puerto Rican or Negro children are not welcome in certain clubs or churches or social groups even in cosmopolitan New York. The complex patterns of approved and disapproved social relationships require a continuing learning, even if one refuses to abide by the approved patterns.

In addition, every person is automatically a part of a vast complex of *indirect* relationships to a socioeconomic class, to a tribe, community, region, town, state, and nation. As he grows older the forms and meanings of these relationships will change. He will need to relearn the implications of his social relationships when he is old enough to vote, or when he moves from laborer to foreman to manager to director.

All social relationships are also influenced by *age*, and in some instances the associations made, and the learning required, are directly related to age—whether in required school attendance, being drafted into the Armed Forces, or when obliged to retire.

Some social relationships are determined by *activity*, whether in work, recreation, religious association, benevolent or social action, political party, or union. An individual may be in many of these or may relate to very few activity groups. Within each group are complex changing relationships that require continued learning for everyone involved if the groups are to fulfill their varied functions.

Social relationship may be "given" or "chosen." The person cannot change his family heritage or his community and national origin. In many instances he can move to another community or nation, and this involves the learning of new relationships. Among activity groupings there is more frequent change according to the decisions of participants, but these moves also involve new learning.

Capacities. If a person never has reason to be dissatisfied with his status and so never seeks to change it, he may never have to learn, consciously, about these social relationships. However, most people, at one time or another, become aware of the implications of their social status. Such understanding may depend primarily on a sensitivity to all the threads that weave them into the social fabric, and of the damage that may be done in attempting to tear that fabric. In some societies the patterns are harmful rather than beneficial, so that basic social changes are needed before stability of internal relationships can be viable and effective.

The capacity for learning relationships or learning about social relationships is one of awareness and sensitivity to other persons and to the structures within which those relationships are formed or controlled. The explication of these is seldom necessary, but in some occupations—such as management or politics—and on higher levels of group leadership, a sense of the processes of social relationships is essential to success. Of course this sensitivity may be used either to facilitate constructive and cooperative interaction or to manipulate others for one's own advantage.

Social relationships become a matter of explicit learning in sociology, psychology, economics, and other social sciences. The capacity required for responsible work in these disciplines is the same openness and objectivity required in other sciences, though it is recognized that objectivity in such fields cannot be impersonal.

Setting. Every setting in which a person finds himself has some kind of social structure and requires some kind of social relationship. Home, school, business, church, club, community, nation—each is a welter of relationships in gradual or rapid change. The setting of the learning required for successful social relationships may change in part in keeping with aging, but usually what needs to be learned is quite specific and particular. Behavior required to get along in a street gang is very different from the etiquette of the bank's board of directors.

A major distinction can be seen between rural and urban cultures. Rural group relationships tend to be more traditional, conservative, and hierarchical. Urban group relations tend to be more democratic, more subject to change, and more dominated by economic power. Getting along in either setting, therefore, requires continued learning.

Obviously there is a close interrelation between group relationships and other aspects of culture. A person of great artistic ability may, because of that ability, have a very different set of social relationships from a less talented brother. Professional competence may bring social status unavailable otherwise. Still, openness to a changed social grouping does not relieve the mobile person from having to learn the modes of conduct appropriate to, or required by, the groups among which he moves.

Process. Every society has an extensive armory of instruments with which it teaches its members about social relationships. From the point of view of the learner this is primarily imitation of the practices and attitudes around him, and the teacher may be the family, friend, stranger, or boss. From the point of view of the "teacher"—whoever that might be— the primary instruments for teaching are positive and negative social pressures. The appeal of approval for one kind of action, or the fear of ostracism for another kind, are powerful forces to which most people yield most of the time.

Behavior Patterns

Content. Social relationships and behavior patterns are obviously closely related, but they are also distinct ranges of learning. Culture has been given many definitions, but it is most frequently identified with characteristic patterns of behavior. These may be explained in terms of various theories, or may be seen as expressing a basic set of standards for conduct, in which case culture would be defined as the standards by which people determine their behavior.

As with social relationships, so in cultural formation, it is not possible for a person to escape some kind of cultural configuration by the society in which he grows up. Usually the major characteristics of the culture are absorbed before he is verbal, and are continually reconfirmed in everything he does thereafter. Cultural expressions can be identified in modes of family and group life, in patterns of social organization, in forms of collective artistic activity, and in types of occupations. Each of these is given concrete expression in architecture, city structure, sculpture, and tools, and each successive culture leaves its deposit of artifacts by which archaeologists can make rough estimates of the behavior patterns of life in which they were produced.

While each aspect of a culture involves learning—artistic forms, toolmaking, urban planning, construction of buildings —the more basic spirit of a people is learned in a more unselfconscious way, such as kin relations, language, etc. In highly integrated cultures, usually the simpler ones, every aspect of culture helps to express the same spirit, whether in ways of working, ways of behaving, ways of thinking, ways of rearing the young, ways of preserving life, or ways of fighting.

In more advanced, and in more extensive, cultures there is an interrelation between all aspects but less chance of integration into a coherent whole. Such cultures are pluralistic, where behavior patterns must be understood in terms of the wider culture and also of many subcultures. The person who lives in such a pluralistic culture has a more complex set of patterns to learn and to live by.

Capacities. The culture within which a person develops provides a frame for all his thought and action. It is a form of anchor, or fixed reality around which his life revolves until he is able to become self-conscious about its character and influence. But even then there is no way to expunge its influence from his life. He is marked by the culture in which he grew up. Thus it is both a frame or context for development and a set of limits upon that development. There is no way for a child growing up in the Bolivian altiplano to become Japanese without the Bolivian background always showing through. Much as he may wish to change his values, convictions, and patterns of life, it is a Bolivian background from which he is trying to change, and that background has left its mark upon him. Every capacity of a person's life is shaped by his culture; the configuration is total. Because there are so many elements within every large or advanced culture each person has an increasing range of possible responses as he grows older, but the integrity of a culture is expressed in part by its ubiquity of influence.

Setting. Every activity of life provides a setting in which cultural behavior patterns may be learned, for the patterns of the setting are the principal channel by which the culture is propagated. Home, school, work, recreation—each is an expression of the culture, and every social grouping and institution is engaged in its perpetuation.

The only institution that makes a self-conscious effort at a systematic study of cultural behavior patterns is the university, and learning objectively about the culture is the activity of many different academic disciplines. The objectivity necessary may itself be a cultural product; that is, a society may have such a powerful conviction of its own virtue that it cannot allow for an objective and critical examination of those things it holds as ultimate values.

Processes. From the learner's point of view, the process of learning behavior patterns is one of assimilation. Rarely is there an occasion for a person to examine critically his whole cultural frame. The greater the cultural interaction in the world the greater the flow of constant adaptation, but this too is learned by assimilation, usually so gradually that the learner is not aware of the implicit cultural contrasts. Among the many forces precipitating cultural interaction have been trade, religious diffusion, and military conquest. With modern means of instant mass communication this cultural interchange moves much more rapidly, and many of the forms of expression lose their particular cultural context and become intercultural or international.

From the point of view of the "teacher" cultural patterns are propagated by offering limited alternatives of choice. If a particular pattern is the only one a person meets in early life, it is the only one he has any possibility of adopting. Since he has to live by some pattern, he will adopt (though there is a possibility that he will contribute to it or alter it) the cultural pattern under which he has grown up.

MORAL RULES

Content. The term "moral" is used here in the broad sense both of social and of personal conduct. Moral and ethical codes are often developed around religious sanctions, though this is not inherently necessary. Every society develops value judgments on types of conduct, with approved actions being moral and disapproved actions being immoral. Man is an inherently moral creature, so it is impossible for a person to grow up in any society without being exposed to concepts of right and wrong. When these concepts have their base within the framework of the society—established and maintained by certain individuals or a power structure—there can be no appeal against them except by moving outside the social setting. On the other hand, when the base of moral concepts is a universal or transcendent conviction about man and that which transcends him, then there is a built-in basis of appeal against any particular moral judgment. In these circumstances both the basis of the code and the particular items of conduct it approves or disapproves must be learned.

Older societies develop long legal traditions. Moral learning may require knowledge of vast stores of legislation and of decisions of the courts in the interpretation of that legislation. The legal profession is, in part, a social instrument for the clarification of public morality and the police are, in part, the social instrument for enforcing public morality. Thus some members of society are expected to acquire professional competence for the development and enforcement of moral and ethical codes.

Moral and ethical judgments are implied in nearly every form of human activity. They may be interpreted as etiquette or sportsmanship or the pragmatic practice of the road, but beyond this are codes of honor in different vocations, business ethics, political morality, national morality, and the whole range of the professional study of ethics. Social relations may be interpreted in moral terms, and in all social groupings there tend to be approved codes between members distinct from codes of conduct in relation to outsiders. Distinctive moral patterns are one particular expression of subcultural differences. Orthodox religious groups may have very strict moral prohibitions as one aspect of their self-identity, maintained in part to prevent assimilation with less orthodox neighbors. A neighborhood teen-age gang may have a code that helps to distinguish it from other gangs or from the world around. Throughout life, then, there is pressure for continued learning about moral conduct. As moral practices change, tension is created between one's previous moral teachings and what one sees happening to him.

An internal consequence of pressure for moral conformity within social groups is the encouragement of guilt feelings that can lead to psychological disturbances if the expected conduct by two communities in which one participates differs too sharply.

Capacities. Moral learning is intended to develop within each individual a "sense" of right and wrong, a sense of responsibility to the code and guilt feelings as an internal compass guiding to right conduct. The pressure of society is upon the conduct, regardless of the rationalization an individual may make on his own for the way he will act. When moral codes have a religious base, the learning of moral conduct may involve an elaborate process to explain the source of the moral ideas and the reasons for their present forms. In many instances this requires a capacity for deductive reasoning from principle to specific application. This may be elaborated in some cultures into an extensive tradition of legal interpretations and adaptations each of which seeks its validation in some earlier precedent. In others, less effort is made to teach background and principles, for particular patterns of conduct are implemented directly. Still these must be "learned" in their own way by each individual, whether or not he observes them in his own conduct.

Setting. The primary source of moral teaching and learning is in the family, for the moral code of the community is first presented, interpreted, and supported or opposed in a situation where the person has no defense or basis of choice. Formation takes place here through the action of parents, siblings, friends, and acquaintances. Tremendous pressure can be brought to bear upon a child in such a way that he will be marked for life. When this moral teaching is integrated with strong religious teaching (particularly with transcendent bases of reward and punishment) a person may never be able to make a responsible moral decision on his own without profound feelings of guilt. Thus the teaching of the first few years is part of the lifelong pattern or setting by which a person faces new moral learning or new tests of his moral commitment.

The various communities in which a person participates usually imply their own moral codes, as noted above, and the level of loyalty or dependence upon these can be a powerful factor in encouraging or suppressing new learning in ethical and moral matters.

Explicit teaching about moral and ethical matters is usually a part of every school program—public school, private school, church school, or university. Human conduct is a matter for study and discussion in courses in history, literature, the arts, politics, economics, law, journalism, etc. The way these subjects are handled, and the influence of the teacher and other students, can have an important influence on moral and ethical understanding. A school's moral influence is not limited to the classroom, however, but is expressed also in administrative and organizational structures, the level and patterns of student responsibility, the activities of the playing field and of student organizations. Each can provide a setting of moral and ethical influence and learning. Some disciplines are devoted specifically to the study of conduct, such as law, ethics, and moral philosophy.

Moral and ethical codes do not exist in isolation from other aspects of life, but are closely intertwined with concepts of bodily development, of social relations, ideological ascriptions, and philosophical understanding. Man is always set in a situation of moral and ethical decision, for he must act in order to live, and every action has moral and ethical dimensions.

Process. From the point of view of the learner, moral conduct is learned primarily by trial and error, particularly in early years. As a person grows older more of his moral and ethical learning is conducted through anticipation, observation, and discussion. From the point of view of the "teacher" moral learning is accomplished by rewards and punishments, which begin very early in life in smiles and frowns to an infant, but may lead to society's threat of taking the life of a criminal who has broken sufficiently significant norms of conduct. All along the line in between there are innumerable ways by which individuals and groups reward or punish good and bad conduct. This process is highly complex in a mobile and open society because each individual is always at the intersection of many differing moral pressures, and every choice must be a conditional and relative one. Action that brings approval of schoolteachers may be condemned by parents; action approved by the Army sergeant may be condemned by one's church; action approved by the boss at the office may break a federal law; action approved by fraternity members may be disapproved by sorority members. Without a common absolute or transcendent frame of reference, both for knowing what is right and wrong and also for the rewarding and punishing of such action, no modern society can overcome the complex tensions between the moral codes each person is subjected to in the course of daily life. And even when there is an acknowledged transcendent frame of reference the problems of interpretation and application may be equally diverse and conflicting. Thus the rewarding and punishing are ambiguous "teachers" and even under a religiously oriented transcendent frame of reference, it is possible for a conscientious and pious person to look around and observe, "I was dismayed when I saw the prosperity of the wicked." [20]

Ideological Ascription

Content. The term "ideology," [21] as used today, refers to a view of the world by which a person finds a meaningful place for himself and his commitments. Original Marxian theory is unable to explain the world as a present-day Communist sees it, so a new Communist ideology is developing which attempts to put together in a meaningful way the multiple facets of reality. Similarly, others who hold different philosophical positions need to find ways to see the meaning of life. An ideology operates on a level more immediately related to daily living than one's basic theological or philosophical commitments. It may be described, in a sense, as the range of middle principles that give guidance to immediate loyalties and actions. It is in this sense that the term is employed here.[22]

Most societies have built their patterns of thought and commitment around ideologies that rationalize or justify their existence. Each person is expected to become familiar with, and to adopt, the ideology of his society if he is to be an acceptable member. Refusing to accept that ideology leads in

some cases to ostracism, and in others to incarceration or ex-
pulsion. The accepted ideology may be passed on from generation to generation through myths and stories or may be
explicitly formulated in school studies. Its content is essentially
the account of the origin of the social body and its early development, and to the spirit of that origin and development
the member of society is expected to be true.

Ideology includes the kind of introduction to nationalism
expressed in speeches on patriotic holidays so attractive to
children, in patriotic acts in schools and military forces, in
courses on history in lower schools. Similarly, ideology finds
expression in the teaching in churches and religious communities with their particular views of the world. Most children, thus, are exposed at one time or another to ideologies
to which they are expected to ascribe if they are to be acceptable members of their group, community, or nation.

An ideology may include the meaning, the legacy, and the
ambitions of a group or country, and usually emphasizes the
myths which seek to describe its distinctive values. The
description of what it means to be a "democratic country"
would be an essential part of the ideology of the United States,
just as a picture of a "people's republic" would be an essential
part of the ideology of modern China. These descriptions may
or may not be realistic; they are maintained as a vision of the
ideal to which all good citizens give their loyalty.

In large and inclusive societies—such as the Roman Empire and the British Empire—there were many ideologies operating side by side. In harsh dictatorial societies, such as
Spain under the Inquisition or Nazi Germany, there may be a
strenuous effort made by the government to propagate one
official ideology.

An ideology is a collective entity, designed to bring together many individuals into some common enterprise,
whether it is "winning the West," or "saving the benighted
heathen," or "making the world safe for democracy." It is an
operating entity, and requires action or the appearance of ac-

tion to keep it alive. For most people it is only a latent idea in peacetime, but it is brought quickly to the surface in times of danger or stress. Similarly, for most people it is dormant when they are far from centers of power, but for those close to important decision-making, in government or industry or educational institutions, ideology takes on greater importance. Most issues of conflict in power centers reflect conflicting ideologies as operative patterns, for from one's ideology is derived the direction for what should be done. Ideological ascription is not a natural growth; it must be "learned."

Capacities. Since some ideological mortar is necessary to bind any group together, every member of a group needs the capacity to respond by some level of ascription to the accepted ideology of the group. If acceptance is to be maintained with intensity over a long period of time, an accepting attitude and a readiness for intellectual conformity are essential. Ideological ascription assumes loyalty not so much to the group as to what the group stands for, to its cause, to its future, and to its meaning. Such ascription is usually necessary, if the group is a voluntary one, as a basis for financial support. Thus voluntary organizations usually engage in an annual reaffirming of ideological loyalty at the time the budget needs to be raised. For the nation, patriotism is tested not only in time of war but also in times of great or rapid change, when the ideology must be described in new terms or given a new setting.

For some people, then, an ideological ascription is a once-in-a-lifetime act of acceptance. For others, maturity or new experiences or schooling raise questions about prior commitments and may lead to sharp changes in ideology. Thus in this range it is possible for two kinds of learning to come into play. One which is essentially an acceptance of what is offered, without questioning; the other an active, critical, responsible choosing of stance.

Setting. Since an ideology is a collective concept, and is one aspect of relationship to larger groupings—church or faith or nation or political affiliation—the setting for learning an ideology is an active encounter with such groupings. Every type of collective conviction is related directly or indirectly to the group's ideology, though there is seldom occasion for individuals in the group to think explicitly about those relationships except when the group or nation is under stress.

Schools are agencies both for promoting and for questioning the validity of ideologies. A university may promote an ideology in which it sees its own significance "writ large" in society, and in which other "estates" are relatively unimportant. At the same time the university may be a place where all ideologies are scrutinized from different philosophical or theological perspectives. This kind of critical examination, with the possibility of revising or changing one's ideology, usually comes later in life and requires a social setting in which the university has considerable freedom. The only other occasion for change of ideology is when an ideology fails, when it is obviously unable to explain what is happening.[23] Events beyond the control of the group or nation thus can have a powerful and formative influence on ideological learning.

Clearly there is a close relation between cultural patterns and ideological affirmations, and there may be an equally close relation between ideology and morality, so that the learning in one range is likely to affect the learning in another. However, an ideology is not necessary in the same sense as are social relations, cultural patterns, or moral codes. It is possible for a person to have no active ideology in any self-conscious sense, even though he lives among people who do make such affirmations.

Process. From the point of view of the "learner," the way one learns one's ideology is by guided rationalization. Thinking, particularly early in life, as a critical rational activity, is not necessary. One is to believe and accept what some authority—parent, teacher, priest—tells him he should think.

From the point of view of the "teacher," an ideology is

implanted by indoctrination. It is of the very nature of ideologies that they are to be passed on from group to individual or from generation to generation as the obvious and "right" things to believe and hold. For this reason there is no need to suggest alternatives or hold the dogma up for critical examination. The function of the ideological teacher is to show the inadequacy of any other view suggested. In some repressive societies fear is added to indoctrination, whether fear of one's soul being lost in hell for being an apostate, or fear of reprisal from agencies of a police state.

However, for the person moved primarily by fear in his public ideological ascription, there may be within himself a totally different view which can never be expressed, because it would be unhealthy to do so under his present circumstances. Thus there is a great deal of hypocrisy in all groups devoted to ideals for church or society or nation when their members are unable to make clear that their private convictions do not conform with the implications of their public actions. When this conflict between private commitment and public action is self-conscious, it may be an evidence of new learning about one's view of the world, it may be a rationalization for psychological problems generated in the individual's relation to the group, or it can be the occasion for a basic rethinking of his commitments and beliefs.

RELATION TO NATURE

Content. The physical universe to which a person is exposed varies sharply in different parts of the earth. The Andean Indians learn types of activity because of altitude and air pressure which differ sharply from the Amazon jungle Indians a few miles to the east. Eskimos and Bali women depend on "nature" in very different ways, in dress, in preparation of food, in social relationships, largely because of the great difference in the type of physical nature that surrounds them. Every person is born into a physical environment that is natural as well as social. His relation to nature must be learned, and when he moves from place to place that relationship changes. Man's dependence upon the particular order of nature around him is obvious in relation to time, for when he changes time zones his interior "time clocks" must readjust.

Much of man's learning about physical nature is devoted to overcoming its control over his life; now highly technical societies are able to provide "conditioned environment" by which a person may be totally isolated from time measured by sunrise or sunset, and seasons marked by summer or winter. Still every person is related to nature and dependent upon natural processes of his own body. He may be unaware of many aspects of this dependence, yet when there is the occasion to reflect upon that relationship or to learn about one's physical surroundings, the content of what is to be learned is limitless. It includes all the obvious facts that may be deduced from simple observations as well as the phenomena that can be studied only by highly sophisticated equipment or thought about only on the highest theoretical levels. Terms that indicate such esoteric dimensions of this range of learning as quasars, the red shift, antibodies, neutrons, laser, are glibly used in popular conversation. However, people who can speak knowingly of such advanced scientific developments might be totally helpless under circumstances which Eskimos find ordinary and routine. What one learns about nature, therefore, may vary greatly according to the region in which one lives, the kind of society one shares, and one's occupational requirements and interests. In university or research laboratory it might require esoteric theories unimaginable to men who have developed great skills in wresting a living from the most unfavorable natural environments, such as the Kalahari Desert in Africa.

Capacities. There may be many different reasons or motives for learning about nature, requirements for survival, facilities for pleasure, or inspiration for the arts. Each of these in turn influences the capacity necessary for learning. Though "science" is the principal way modern man attempts to learn the "laws" of nature in order to "control" his physical surroundings, for the far longer span of man's history he learned about nature from direct observation without the cumulative theoretical base that is now called science. Fascinating conjectures have been proposed in attempts to describe how the "firsts" took place—the first fire, the first roast beef, the first dam, the first wheel. These events cannot be recaptured, but there is ample record among contemporary societies of the understanding and use of nature without the theoretical or experimental tools of "science." Thus learning about nature requires two kinds of capacity: one, the capacity for observation, experimentation, and adaptation; the other, the capacity for theoretical, logical thinking, controlled inference, and creative hypothetical constructs. Ultimately learning facts about nature depends upon what one accepts as a "fact" and its verification. This capacity is largely dependent upon the social setting of such learning.

Setting. Every place is a setting for learning about physical nature, though what may be learned varies according to the characteristics of the natural surrounding, and according to the facilities for such learning. An urban child has very different things to learn at different stages of life than does a child of the jungle. What may be necessary for survival in one place may be unheard of in another. Thus the setting may determine the content of expected learning as well as the available facilities. Without a telescope very different things will be learned about celestial bodies than where advanced astronomical observation is part of a social heritage. Similarly, religious or metaphysical views may so control the observational process that what is learned is a deduction from fixed ideological commitments rather than inductive reasoning from empirical observation. Spiritism which ascribes a being to each rock or tree will lead one of its believers to "learn" distinctive things from the phenomena of wind, rain, sunshine, and the seasons which others would never suspect. The social setting in which a person is reared and his place in the historical process of man's accumulation and dissemination of knowledge about the physical universe largely determines what and how he will learn.

Processes. In identifying the capacities for learning about nature the processes by which this learning takes place have already been indicated. Observation, memory, hypothesizing, and experimenting are the processes by which facts about nature are "known." Undergirding such knowledge have always been the basic drives of man for survival and security. Among some men, and on some levels of human development in certain periods of history, there has been curiosity about nature which led to the discovery of knowledge beyond necessity. In those men and in those periods man's conception of the universe has been expanded beyond his immediate comprehension.

From the point of view of the teacher the processes of learning about nature are demonstration, the encouragement of experimentation, the questioning of inferences, and the interpretation of prior experience. From the point of view of the learner, the processes are problem-solving, trial and error, and the exercise of imagination.

TECHNICAL SKILLS

Content. All technical skills are learned, for each takes a form that is an expression of the culture in which it emerges. Canoe-making was a highly developed skill among the Pacific Coast Indians of North America as it was among the Melanesians, yet the different techniques used were expressions of the great cultural and geographical differences between the two peoples. Unless some natural catastrophe breaks the chain of continuity, technical learning is cumulative.[24] One does not need to learn to drive an automobile with manual shift before learning to drive a car with an automatic transmission. Whether gradually or rapidly, improvement of techniques moves in only one direction and is not usually reversed. Thus each technical skill is specific.

Techniques of making and doing things have an almost limitless range, and include all kinds of physical abilities of which mankind is capable, plus the extension of those abilities by the use of tools, which also range from the simple lever to the sophisticated computer. Skills are not only physical, they can include managerial and administrative activities, artistic, and mental, as well. Some of these are closely related to bodily development—few ballet dancers are fat and few basketball players are short. Certain mental capacities, such as mathematical skill, "come" very easily to some people and not to others. Every kind of work requires a measure of technical skill, and in every society there are processes for passing on needed skills from one generation to another.

A profession is a field of work requiring particular technical proficiency developed under supervision and exercised within a code of practice and ethics established by qualified members of the profession. Learning the various things required for professional competence may be very different for a social worker and an engineer, a clergyman and a surgeon. A century ago there were only three or four recognized professions—teacher, clergyman, doctor, and lawyer. Now thousands of occupations are considered, or claim, to be professions. This claim reflects an effort to elevate the quality and status of many occupations. Whatever the merits of the claim, it is clear that professional competency includes certain standards for the exercise of technical knowledge and skill, and a particular relation between a professional and his clients. "Professional" connotes a certain level of responsibilitiy, both to his field and to the public he serves.[25]

Capacities. Techniques are of so many different kinds, that the physical or mental skills required to perform them are of an equally wide range. They may, however, fall into two kinds of categories. One of these is the development of specific specializations. The acrobat who makes his living standing on his right index finger for two minutes, three times a day at the circus, has developed a very highly specific specialization. The women who sort by sizes the hose brought to them from the knitting machine have developed a specific specialization. The same is true of the man who buffs the polish on new cars as they come through the production line. On the other hand, there are what might be called "logical" skills, which require the putting together of many parts into a complex process or structure. Illustrations of this might be the contractor for a building, the field commander in the army, the administrator of an industry, or the operator of the control tower of an airport. Whether specific or general every one of these skills must be taught and learned.

Each profession involves a set of specific skills that may not be transferred, but must be learned in keeping with the structure of the discipline or nature of the field. Most professions assume a capacity for self-discipline and striving toward perfection of technique or comprehensiveness of knowledge. Often this requires great patience, and equally often creative imagination in meeting new situations. In addition, most professions encourage the capacity to integrate the various skills that are essential to a particular field. Professional training usually seeks to develop an appropriate professional attitude as well as necessary skills.

Settings. The learning of technical skills is often directly related to a particular setting. The simple necessities of daily living—preparing food, getting to and from work, and recreation—all require skills that are learned in the setting of the home, office, school, or playing field. Some technical skills must be learned in school or university where the principles can be formally and systematically introduced and where laboratories are available for practice. In some occupations the developments are so rapid that specific technical skills must be learned in the setting of industry or in the field. Now a new setting outside the organized processes of production (though depending on highly sophisticated industrial production) is the operations in nuclear physics, advanced mathematics, "the conquest of space," and astronomy, in which the most highly sophisticated technical skills are a standard requirement. On this frontier there are no "teachers" because the activities being carried on are essentially creative and experimental.

Most professions now require training in special schools in which the setting is largely controlled. Yet in many instances the student is required to spend time in fieldwork or internship or other kinds of supervised practice before he is considered professionally prepared. Professional schools in the major established professions are often responsible only for initial orientation or introduction to the field. The future surgeon moves from the medical school to the teaching hospital and advances in his field as he participates in operation after operation which are observed and discussed in postoperative conferences with other surgeons. For the young clergyman, seminary may not complete his training, for he still must meet the requirements of his church before ordination, just as the young lawyer must study to pass bar examinations after graduation from law school. This advanced preprofessional training, in factory or field, may be in settings other than the professional school, and since a professional continues to "practice" his profession, the setting of continued learning for the doctor is his office or hospital, for the professor it is his classroom or laboratory, and for the politician it is the legislative chamber.

Process. From the point of view of the learner technical learning is a process of problem-solving, following the well-known steps of problem clarification, hypothesis, testing, and experimentation. This applies in learning how to hold a golf club as it does in learning how to grind a lens. Thousands of technical skills are required to maintain the tools and machinery of modern technological society, and new techniques are being developed every day. However, the new techniques, sophisticated machinery, and technological advances do not eliminate continued use of older techniques of cooking, accounting, or manufacture, so the range of technical learning keeps expanding with mounting rapidity. The way a person learns these multitudes of skills remains the same, whether the skill is mental or physical. Each is designed to develop a process which, once integrated, may be repeated again and again with the same or reliable results.

From the point of view of the teacher, technical skills are developed primarily by demonstration. The process required for a particular skill can be broken down or rationalized into a series of sequential steps, each necessarily following the other. When the necessity of the sequence is understood, and the physical dexterity developed for each step, the technique is learned and can be repeated.

While one may be more comfortable with, and therefore prefer, a particular "way of doing things," modern technology places its value upon a scientific attitude that seeks efficiency in the use of appropriate techniques rather than an emotional commitment to one or another procedure. Thus change itself may become an area of special technical study and skill with the result that change is both expected and sought.

In professions competency is learned, from the point of view of the learner, by relating technical skills to a rational frame of personal and social responsibility. In some professions this may require many years of highly focused training (as in medical specialization) and a sustained personal motivation of interest, expectation of financial benefit, or desire for professional status. Still competency always requires knowledge of the field and skill in using that knowledge in practical ways, whether as an orchestra leader, a professor of history, or an oceanographer. In some professions competency requires the integration of knowledge, skill, understanding, and practice which can be accomplished only after years of experience.

From the teacher's point of view, professional competence is attained by continual application of predetermined standards. Usually this involves passing on to students both the requisite skills and an understanding of the context in which they are to be exercised. Often there is the assumption that a person in the early stages of training is already, somehow, sharing the life of the profession, particularly when field experience implies a commitment to the field involved.

Since there is constant change in the elements of all professions and particularly rapid change in technical professions, there is more and more precedent for continuing education as an essential requirement for professional competency, so that practice, as in medicine, has a dual meaning of learning as well as serving. The able professional must go on learning.

AESTHETIC PREFERENCE

Content. From the day of birth a child is exposed to some forms, patterns, relationships of sense objects, and also to the interpretation of value judgments of those forms made by others around him. He early develops likes or dislikes for certain colors and sounds and shapes. However, his capacity to respond to the sense objects and to their evaluation by others is a natural capacity. If later in life he is able to identify what he dislikes or likes regardless of the taste of others, or to develop an independent aesthetic judgment, this would be an evidence of new learning in the range of aesthetics.

The most common forms for expressing aesthetic taste are the way a person designs useful articles, selects clothes, arranges his home, as well as how he responds to the forms and colors of things around him. His choices may be spontaneous, or the response to a conscious study of art,[26] or the expression of artistic creativity of great sensitivity and sophistication. Thus, aesthetic learning may have three aspects: (*a*) aesthetic appreciation, which includes response to the artistic creation of others, either in listening or looking or in selecting articles for use; (*b*) artistic performance of what others have created, such as producing or acting in a play, dancing a ballet, reading a poem, or playing a piano sonata; (*c*) artistic creation, such as painting a picture, designing a building, composing a symphony, or writing a novel.

Capacities. Obviously some people are born with aesthetic and artistic gifts they do not have to learn. At the age of fourteen Picasso was turned down in his application to the university in Madrid because, the teachers said, there was nothing they could teach him. Nevertheless, such gifts can be developed throughout one's lifetime, as Picasso developed his. He learned from fellow artists and from the world around him, but he was not dependent upon a "teacher" who could pass on to him skills he needed to learn. Aesthetic capacities have to do with sensitivity to form and color and sound. This sensitivity varies in individuals, and is the base upon which other levels of ability depend, though at the initial level it is a responsive type of activity rather than a creative one.

Learning for artistic performance, however, involves skills that need to be nurtured and developed in systematic ways. Teaching and criticism are essential to this development, whether the bodily skills in ballet dancing or the speaking skills in acting. But as these skills are employed in interpretation they shade over into the creative area which can be governed only by the artistic talent of the performer.

Artistic creation requires the courage to shape and reshape the forms and colors and sounds, to which all persons are exposed, according to an inner vision of new forms and colors and sounds. Learning in artistic creation is a subjective activity, often developed in private, yet it is based on sensitivity of response to surroundings on the part of the artist. There is no necessity in artistic learning, nor a logical sequence of steps. Instead it is a range of activity in which sudden inspiration, or leaps of imagination, or flashes of insight from long-delayed reflection find expression. For this reason such artistic learning cannot be anticipated or programmed.

Setting. Aesthetic preference is a general product of participation in a culture. The chalet of Switzerland or the batik houses of Indonesia, the jazz of Harlem, the Westerns of

Hollywood, the styles of Dior or Pucci, the mystical realism of Bergman, the automobile designs of Italy, all have a pervasive influence upon the taste of the populace, and some "learning" is no more than the imitation of fads which come and go. On the popular level this is aesthetic learning, and because of the ubiquity of mass media of communication and world trade these fads are increasingly worldwide in scope.

The long tradition, in creative activity, is that of the followers of a genius, the "schools" around leading artists who initiate new trends and draw to themselves followers of their vision. This often becomes artistic imitation, whether of a Corbusier or of T. S. Eliot. In another period the "school" or "followers" may be attracted to experimentation with new forms so that artistic creation seems to be inspired by nothing more profound than a restless search for the different, justified in terms of the search for new techniques.

Artistic learning has also been institutionalized in formal schooling of many kinds, such as art, dance, writing, and architecture. Shorter terms of teaching are attempted in summer institutes and conferences and in experimental centers. Some of these make a strong impact, such as the Bauhaus, though the impact may often be the result of the dominance of one or a few powerful creative individuals who seek or inspire followers. Usually they are unable to transfer their genius to their students.

Process. From the learner's point of view, then, aesthetic learning is the developing of latent gifts in creative association. From the teacher's point of view it involves prodding, exciting, challenging, and encouraging what cannot be given but only elicited and recognized. Aesthetic capacities defy control and anticipation.

WORLD VIEW

Content. This range of learning could be identified as wisdom, but in a sense wisdom is the result of the use of one's capacities for understanding. Understanding one's world view refers more particularly to the meaning-forming function which people in all societies engage in, though some people do this more explicitly than others.

In simplest terms each act or experience "means" something to every person. The kind of response made to any act, no matter how incidental, is an expression of what that act means to the actor or observer. If he should have occasion to think about it, to try to articulate that meaning, he would be engaging in a simple process of philosophizing. On a higher level a philosopher may examine the meaning of the same act but would employ professional standards of understanding and responsibility. When the meanings of many acts, events, experiences, are put together consciously or unconsciously into a more comprehensive or systematic view of meaning, this may be called a world view.

Understanding of the world and of human existence is the concern of many academic fields, such as art, history, psychology, physics, anthropology, as well as of philosophy and theology. The basic content of these fields, however, is the common experience of all men and women, from the most ignorant to the most educated. And so it often happens that an unschooled, unsophisticated individual may have a more penetrating insight into the meaning of events than a person with advanced specialization in that field. Understanding may appear at any time and place in a person's experience, but it is usually the particular concern of intentional activity on the part of society to produce some individuals with the ability to explicate, formulate, and articulate their world view.

Religious world views have an expanded content because they are based upon an understanding of that which transcends man and his work. The nature of the transcendent frame of reference (the divine), and the way it is to be known, varies according to one's theological position. In some this is accomplished by man's effort; in others knowledge is seen as the result of divine self-revelation.

The difference in type of world view influences the type of capacity required for understanding.

Capacities. Explication, formulation, and articulation of a world view call for the capacity to relate diverse elements and insights into some ordered meaning. In some fields this is a product of rationality and logic, while in others it depends more upon aesthetic sensitivity. The development of a conscious world view, and discussion about it, requires a capacity for abstract thinking. The capacity to relate ideas and experiences indicates an explicit or implicit frame of reference within which the relation can be evaluated or expressed. World-view understanding as meaning-formation involves appreciation and judgment of values in whatever field. Thus understanding implies perspective, so that a change of meaning reflects a change of perspective in parabolic relationship.

Setting. Every context of life influences the meaning-formation of every individual because it helps to shape his experience. Usually conscious efforts to reflect upon what one has "learned" are conducted in the setting of some group effort or school. The distinctive responsibility of the humanities or the liberal arts, as they have been called in the university tradition, has been to provide for reflection upon and the integration of meaning from experience. There are many arguments about the open question of which "arts" are included within the category "liberal," with deep concern at present about whether modern man can be understood apart from the scientific and technological developments of this century.[27] Science is very much a human activity and deserves equal attention with literary and artistic realms in any serious attempt to understand man and the world.

Self-conscious efforts at philosophical understanding have, over many centuries, developed into specific academic disciplines with long traditions of content and methodology. The university attempts to bring a number of disciplines, sometimes organized into different schools, into fruitful mutual exchange, though only occasionally is it possible to find a set of departments or faculties that can operate in different disciplines yet within a common metaphysical or philosophical frame of reference. The seminary is usually accepted as the setting for advanced learning in the area of religious world views, and at one time the theological department of the university was expected to provide the metaphysical system within which the whole work of the university was integrated. The possibility of such unity is becoming less and less in a pluralistic world, so that the institutions attempting to teach world-view understanding must determine their functions on procedural rather than doctrinal grounds. The processes that may contribute to learning world-view understanding can be evaluated in terms of their function but not in terms of the particular stance a person holds at any particular point in the course of his development.

Process. From the point of view of the learner, world-view understanding is gained first through reflection upon his own past experience, the response to new experiences (ideas, events, sensations), the formulation of interpretations of relationship between prior and new experiences, and then the testing of the resulting meanings against the idea of others and future experience. This process of appropriation is individual. No two people can have the same meaning-formation, because the meaning one holds is so directly related to one's "angle of vision" that it is not possible for the meaning to be "transmitted." It can be described, explained, and pointed to, but for each person meaning-formation is a creative act that cannot be duplicated, either between persons or at successive times in the life of any individual.

At all times there is an implicit view of meaning held by every individual, for activity of any kind implies some implicit meaning, and usually that meaning is not explicated until there is an occasion of tension, problem, conflict, or need. On the other hand, there are some individuals for whom meaning is easily articulated, and meaning articulation has a significant function in their daily life. Thus, generally, it would be assumed that philosophical understanding is gained or learned only when it can be articulated. This requires a self-consciousness which is not characteristic of children. Even with self-consciousness such understanding is only a gradual development, fed by the course of exposure and experience which comes to a person in the pilgrimage of his life. So, basically, world-view understanding is an inductive process.

From the point of view of the teacher, such understanding derives from an invitation to the student to share his angle of vision. Historically there has been an assumption that teaching was an activity of transmission of meaning or interpretation, but this is not a possibility for any person. Meaning or interpretation is a function of the interrelationship of ideas and experiences in the complex interaction of an individual, as noted above, and the meaning held by one person cannot be transferred, with its whole set of complex relationships, to another person. The teacher can confront a student with ideas to which he must react, but the reaction cannot be controlled. The teacher can question and challenge each articulation of meaning, but if the answer is determined a priori the process of thinking is truncated. There can be no necessary response, either in tempo or intensity. The distinctive contribution of the teacher is the presentation of another perspective in the light of which the student may reflect upon the meanings he already holds.

There are many ways in which "another perspective" may be brought to bear. Each academic discipline is a perspective upon reality. The historian looks at events from a different perspective than a physicist, and an artist than a theologian, but all may be viewing the same reality. Similarly, within each discipline are different perspectives in terms of different theories: in economics Adam Smith and Keynes differ sharply, in theology Barth and Wieman see things differently, and in art Dali and Wyeth have a different perspective upon the world. These differences stem from the contrasting personal experience and creative capacity of each, the times and places in which they have lived, and thus the influence to which they had the opportunity to respond.

World-view understanding is developed in a continuing dialogue between the diversities of present-day points of view as well as between the present and the past. Repeated efforts are made to establish authority or orthodoxy of certain views, and from time to time great movements of common views converge about these orthodoxies or ideologies. Yet such movements cannot resist change with time, and few of them are able to hold their power over men's minds for very long. The myths on which they are based last much longer than the patterns of meaning ascribed to the myths.

Though this has been a very brief look at ten ranges of learning, it has indicated both the vast quantity and the complexity of what every individual is expected to learn throughout his lifetime. It has indicated, also, the inadequacy of reductionist attempts to find a single process by which a person learns. Realism requires that a person's processes of learning be understood as a complex interaction of the particular matter being considered, his basic mental capacity, the personal background he brings to the occasion, and its sociocultural setting.

Each of the ten ranges is "a piece of a whole" which constitutes the person's lifelong learning, much of which is acquired unconsciously without reflection on its implications for his life. On the other hand, some of this learning is available only with the assistance of another person, though individuals may vary greatly in what they have learned unconsciously or consciously. Each person, therefore, has a different learning profile. See an example of this on the facing page.

What a person learns unconsciously is important to his life but (except in a therapy situation) it cannot be programmed into a social activity. Thus educational activities, which require conscious planning and administration, incorporate those aspects of learning which can be or need to be acquired with

1. Bodily development   ☐ alone

2. Symbol systems   ▨ needing another—informal

3. Social relationships   ⦀ needing another—formal

4. Moral rules

5. Relation to nature

6. Behavior patterns

7. Ideological ascription

8. Technical skill

9. Aesthetic preference

10. World view

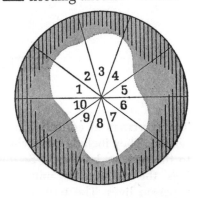

the assistance of other persons either informally or formally.

This extensive review may help clarify an initial issue for all education. Since so much must be learned by each individual in any society, a basic judgment needs to be made as to which things can most effectively be learned alone, which things require the informal aid of others, and which matters can be learned more appropriately in a formal program. There is a perpetual temptation for a society to measure its education by the number of schools and the proportion of its population enrolled in them. But a school separates students—for certain periods of time—from the general community into a special community (the characteristics of such special communities are examined in Chapter IV) on the assumption that such separation is the most effective way to aid the learning of many different matters. The crisis in contemporary education around the world may be, in part, the result of the confusion implicit in that assumption.

Chapter II

SETTINGS

THE CONTEXTS of education are multiple, complex, and inter-related. They include both what is exterior and what is interior to the persons involved. "Setting" usually connotes surroundings, the vicinity, the milieu, the environment within which a person lives. The term will be used in an expanded sense here, referring to the context of education as the totality of what meets a teacher or a school system when a student enters. The setting of education includes all the usual factors of place and time, but also what the student brings inside himself—his experience, his ideas, his habits, his physical endowment, and the deposit of how he has adjusted to all the pressures of life.

Settings may be considered under three formal headings: the *scope* of influences upon participants, indicated in essentially quantitative terms both externally and internally; the character or *quality* of those influences; and the *dynamics*, the direction of movement of circumstances. All three of these may be operative both directly and indirectly, and all are important for understanding what may or may not take place in an educational activity.

SCOPE

Every person is produced, in part, by the worlds he inhabits. "World" may imply a unitary or integrated environment, yet every person exists in a number of worlds each of which attempts to establish its own independence and integrity. Each person shares in creating his own "world" by the factors in his environment which he is willing to take into account in his life and the decisions he makes about them. Thus one can speak of the world of music, or the banking world, or the world of sports. In this sense the world is a set of environmental elements and activities to which a person is related and which provide identification and meaning for him. In reality, of course, all these worlds are interrelated, but this interrelationship of their worlds is not obvious in the experience of most people. The other worlds (or the rest of the world) intrude upon what they are tempted to think is a unitary environment.

The scope of environmental influences, therefore, may be seen as a series of concentric circles stretching out in every direction from each individual. The nearest circle is that of the immediate family, which is the bearer of some racial and cultural heritage, a style of life, patterns of conduct, levels of taste, and a set of personal relationships between various members of the family group.

Exterior

In some societies the family is in intimate and continuous contact with the extended family so that there is little awareness, on the part of a child, of differences between brother and cousin or father and uncle. In more mobile societies, the "extended family" may be so far away that there is little sense of relationship or belonging—he visits Uncle Ben only on holidays. In such a setting the grouping of close friends fulfills the functions of the extended family, often with continuous and intimate relating of all of life's activities. Thus what a child thinks and does may be as strongly influenced by the neighbor next door as by the father. Such a relationship, of course, depends upon the openness of the whole family to such close friends.

The next step in the enlarging circle of environment is the forming of friendships by each member of the family on his own, not limited to the family group. These friendships, sometimes made in early years and lasting through life, may be the most powerful formative influence in the life of a person. Such friendships may be independent of other groupings or they may be set in the context of gangs, or associational relationships which add further cement to the relationships. Again, some of these associational relationships may be derived from family that "belongs" to a country club, a union, a church, the farm bureau, or a vacation community. The children in such settings are brought into association with others, not by their own choice but by family decision. Such "nonfriends" may be as influential in their lives as "friends." School would provide a similar kind of larger association, either chosen by parents or with attendance required by the community. Here a person is brought into active contact and relationship of various kinds, with people beyond the circle of friendship and group association. The school, in this sense, is a reflection of the neighborhood in which a child grows up. Being in a particular neighborhood exposes a person to the different kinds of people, to the events of community life, to the consequences of its geographical location and economic level, to the kinds of work men do, the kinds of houses they live in, the kinds of street life that characterize the town or city, and to the kinds of recreation available.

In an urban center there may be a variety of neighborhoods or communities to which a person is exposed—one where he lives, another where he goes to school, another where he shops, another where he works, and yet another where he goes for recreation. In small-town or rural communities, particularly in less mobile societies, all these activities would be shared by the same people in a common setting.

Every neighborhood or community is influenced by the region in which it is set. With differences of geography— mountains, pampas, seacoast—come differences of industry and transportation, of racial and cultural patterns. The region may be part of a nation, as in the larger nations of the world, or it may include several countries with differences of national histories and loyalties. Beyond the region is the nation or group of nations which constitute yet another circle of the setting of any individual or institution. And from the mid-twentieth century onward in time every person is exposed to every event in every country and continent on earth—and in space beyond. Thus the setting of every individual is universal in scope and includes everything that is happening in the world.

In attempting to discern the implications of the scope of settings in which a person lives, one needs to make a distinction between direct participation and indirect influence. Every person must act to live, but most persons tend to respond to a much larger scope of environment than they participate in, just as the vocabulary they comprehend is much larger than the vocabulary they employ. Yet vicarious influences are often as great, and can be greater, than the influence of participation, particularly for a retiring person.

Similarly, a distinction can be made between the direct and indirect influences of one's setting. The person who grows up in the home of a farmer who wants his son to be a farmer and will give him financial backing only if he goes into the same occupation has a direct pressure upon him which can be countered only by a greater influence to get off the farm. However, if he grows up in a suburban family where the father commutes to work in the city and therefore he never sees the things his father does or how they fit into the total operation of the company, the influence of the father's occupation would be indirect, yet it may be equally formative upon his life. Or the indirect influence may be seen in a person who lives in a society where an improvident government attempts to live beyond its resources. Although the citizen had nothing to do with the economic decisions of the government, he suffers along with all other citizens in the consequent inflation. Thus it is possible to describe the larger scope of the setting in which whole societies or nations exist and discern the implications of those settings for educational processes.

The scope of settings may be described from the person outward. It is equally valid to see the lines of influence moving from macrocosm to microcosm. The forces of a "civilization," such as the Chinese or the Western, have been at work over such long periods of history that they shape every aspect of life. Describing from the inside out may give the impression that the larger sweep of influences may be accepted or rejected, that they are conditional, but this is not the case. An individual has no choice as to whether he will be born into, and therefore shaped and configured by, one civilization or another. And that shaping influence is pervasive. He may be exposed, sometime during his lifetime, directly to the patterns of another civilization, but he cannot respond to them *de novo*. If he moves from Peking to New York, he will respond to the new environment in terms of his configurations in the Chinese background. So the influence of the settings upon education must be seen first in terms of the larger cultural configurations of which educational enterprises, as well as the students and faculty, are a part.

Interior

What "interior setting" can an educator expect to find in a student arriving for school? A teacher may know the theories and findings of psychologists, and the interpretations of philosophers, but when Mary or José or Wong stands before him he can make no assumptions about the particularity of that person. He has to find out, if he can, what native physical and intellectual capacities that particular person has, how experiences have shaped his life, and how events have been interpreted and reinterpreted. Only in special circumstances can a teacher probe beneath the surface with psychoanalytic procedures; most of his insights into each student must come by observing behavior and listening to what the student says. His

philosophy (even theology) and his own psychological understanding may alert the teacher for things to watch for, but if
he is to be fair to the student, he will always be checking his
generalizations or prior expectations against the evidence of
his own observation.

Whatever the teacher may draw upon to help him understand students, he must recognize that each individual has a
particular history, and carries his own personal interpretation
of that history. Each individual is a unique personality, and
the distinctiveness of his personality describes the interior
setting that the educator meets in any educational occasion.

Obviously the uniqueness is less a physiological than a historical fact. It is in the way a person puts together (consciously
or unconsciously) what has happened to him, the meanings
events have had for him, the ideas to which he has been exposed, and the feelings he has about all of these, that the inner
profile has been drawn.[28] No student could be conscious of all
the aspects of his interior setting, and no teacher can ever
discern all the elements that constitute a student's personality.
Yet teachers must realize that those undiscerned reservoirs of
feeling and meaning still may have a formative influence on
what a student can appropriate out of his educational experiences. So teachers in their turn observe the phenomena of the
classroom and are continually engaged in interpreting and
reinterpreting the personalities and situations of students, just
as students are interpreting and reinterpreting the educational
activities in which they happen to have been engaged. Thus
while a teacher may be attempting to "locate" the setting of
a student, that interior setting is continually changing. Personality has structure and continuity, but the tempo of change
in its shape and expression keeps time with changes in its
total situation.

The unity and integrity of a person's internal setting may be
difficult to discern because each person can respond in a variety of ways to things, events, ideas, persons and groups to
which he is exposed. The pattern of his thinking may be

broken by a crisis which, at this moment, elicits a response that no one could anticipate. Whatever the expression of the moment, the vast complex store of his internal setting is as "real" as the geographical setting of his community or nation.

The distinctive concern of all kinds of education, in all ranges of learning, points beyond behavior to ideas. Bodily development requires some idea of health as well as good muscle tone, and cultural configuration involves ideas of cultural patterns as well as the appropriate behavior. Educators are never satisfied only with imitations of actions; they press beyond to articulation in order both to suggest the meaning of the act and to discover whether the student understands what has been done. Teachers try to find out whether what is being done openly and consciously in an educational occasion has any relationship to or consequences in a student's interior setting. The only means by which the teacher can go beyond observing behavior is by articulation. Thus education always seeks some way to relate articulation with appropriation. But a one-to-one relationship is never possible because appropriation is a slow dialectical process, whereas articulation may be prompt and facile. Yesterday's events shape the way a person is able to understand what happens today, and at the same time what happens today and tomorrow will lead to a reinterpretation of yesterday, and the day before.[29] It is not possible for a person to see immediately the implications for his whole life of a particular experience.[30] Each experience, particularly heightened dramatic experiences, enter the stream of interpretation and may be reworked time and again as future events give occasion for seeing new meanings for them. A crisis, such as the death of a mother, may have a very different meaning to a boy when he is twelve than it has for him when he looks back to that event twenty or forty years later. Similarly, less critical experiences change in meaning as a person moves forward in the pilgrimage of his life. Every person has a "map" in the background.[31]

The historic way by which educational agencies have chosen

to consider the ideas which a student brings, and the ideas he meets in the educational program, has been to collect them into academic disciplines, such as mathematics, geography, history, and physics. However, within the student these ideas cannot be so clearly compartmentalized. The student has (usually unconsciously) integrated his ideas into a more or less amorphous collection of knowledge and interpretation with which he approaches the educational occasion. The interpretation of life which he brings is a complex interaction of ideas about reality—objects, events—and his ideas about their significance, value, or meaning; and this meaning (whether he can articulate it or not) expresses his world view.

QUALITY

The exterior setting from which a student comes and the interior setting he brings to an educational experience always have a distinctive character. The kind of family or gang with which a boy associates is as important as is the fact that he has been in a family or a gang, and the quality of such experiences is an important factor in how he will study, what he will think about, as well as what learning means to him. If he comes from a hard, demanding, unloving family situation, he has a heavy burden to overcome in relating normally with people who are not hard, demanding, and unloving. If the gang with which he associated had low artistic taste and moved in a community that offered no opportunity for artistic expression, he will be aesthetically deprived. If he comes from a culture that places a very low value on physical labor, it would be difficult to develop a different attitude toward work.

Geographically, for instance, has the experience of the person been in one small rural community, one narrow mountain valley, or one slum barrio for all of his life; or has he traveled widely and been exposed to circumstances and people of different regions and cultures?

In material things a person may come from a wealthy home

or a poor one, on any one of the nine levels from lower-lower
to upper-upper, and the type of poor or wealthy home will
make a significant difference in his response to any educational
opportunity. A person may be rich in facilities for recreation
yet poor in facilities for meeting people of different cultures.
He may have sufficient food but no books to read. What is the
character of his material background?

The character of his emotional environment, the stability or
instability of parental influence and family life, the kind of
community spirit and exposure, the kinds of friendships formed
and the nature of the associations maintained—each of these
can qualify the character of the setting that a student brings
to his educational experience.

Every environment has some aesthetic expression. It may be
a slum of cardboard shacks or a slum of regal old homes. It can
be a community devoted to a particular style of architecture
or a particular form of music. It can be a region that rejects
all artists as worthless or one in which artists occupy a place of
special affection. Whichever, the aesthetic character of the
community is a crucial formative factor in the life of each
person.

And each person lives in some kind of intellectual atmos-
phere, where the intellect is highly cultivated or suspect,
where there are many or few opportunities for intellectual
stimulation. The intellectual activities of a family, or school,
or community may be highly sophisticated but very parochial;
they may be widely inclusive but very superficial. A person
may grow up in a university community and be exposed to
the arena of conflicting thought and commitment, or in the
same community he may only visit the hamburger joint and
cheap movies.

The character of the exterior setting has a counterpart in
the interior setting, for the first influence of these various environmental factors is the way the person responds to them
(either incorporating or rejecting each one) and the interpretation he makes of their meaning for himself. He may de-

velop a lifelong drive to overcome childhood poverty, or he may want to settle down and "never go anywhere." He may like the music he hears at home day after day, or he may be glad to escape from reading to play baseball, or he may resent the pressure of his gang to do so. Since the interior response of an individual cannot be predicted, the total interrelationship of the external and internal character of the setting must always be open for reappraisal.

DYNAMICS

The external and internal settings of a learner are never static. Both the external and internal setting are caught in the currents of historical development. No matter how somnolent a small town, when a former resident returns after years away he sees at once that "the old place has changed." And it has, but so has he, and it would look different to him even if nothing had changed in the town. The setting of education cannot be understood except in dynamic terms; the conditions are not the same at any two moments. Geographical and economic circumstances do not stand still; neither do cultural and intellectual factors. Each individual is in continuous dynamic movement and is not the same person today as he was yesterday or will be tomorrow.

The currents of the settings may be viewed in terms of the direction of change as well as the depth of change. The inhabitants of a region may not be aware of gradual industrial development of a nearby river valley, yet the shift of economic activity, the rise or fall of population, the changes in land use, may be tokens of a cultural change that will eventually affect all ranges of learning for each individual in the region as profoundly as would a sudden and highly visible change in political policy.

Each person deals with these changes around and within him by continual adjustment and reinterpretation. Each person puts together the pressures of different ranges of learning in a distinctive way, and does so repeatedly in terms of the totality of what is happening to him, and of the rate, direction, and depth of the currents in which he is caught. At any time a person may be totally preoccupied with a problem of bodily development, or of developing a technical skill. At those times all other aspects of life take a lesser place in his attention, and at those times he may be most open to "learning" in those ranges. Openness, as a factor of his total situation influenced by a constellation of interacting pressures and concerns, is also a dynamic concept. It must be seen in terms of times or occasions. Each person is caught in the tension between stability and the dynamics of life, so openness to learning may be described as a movement to reestablish equilibrium between inertia and change. Since the setting always includes both objective reality and a person's interpretation of it, no two persons can occupy the same setting. Each person exists in a distinctive, ever-changing setting.

Everything a person experiences influences his life pattern. This influence cannot be predicted in advance, nor can it be measured at any one time afterward. The currents within which all experiences are set and in which all responses are made mean that the consequence of an experience changes as the experience is interpreted and reinterpreted.

In human affairs, every element of circumstance is a pressure or force playing upon each individual and he must deal with it by responding in some way. In large arenas of human affairs this pressure may be seen as a "challenge" [32] to which a society must respond, but "challenge" is too dramatic a word for the pressure of poverty on a five-year-old, or of life in a highly sophisticated literary family upon a ten-year-old, or of living by the sea upon a fifteen-year-old. These pressures may work blatantly or subtly upon the ideas, fears, hopes, imagination, ambitions of the person. All will reflect in his educational activity. To know the settings out of which a person comes provides clues for investigation, but studies of settings that do not also cover the responses made by the person to his situation are of little value except to provide statistics to play with.

No matter how far in the past a child may have had an unpleasant experience with a teacher or been excited over the discovery about a natural process, or understood for the first time an insight into human behavior, the whole catalog of his past experiences and responses is part of the present intersection at which he stands and is engaged in understanding their interaction.

The person who comes to an educational occasion bears experiences and his response to them; he also bears patterns of thinking and acting by which he has responded to the events and structures of his environment. The educator meets all of this when he meets a student. The primary problem for a teacher is to understand each student's complex exterior and interior setting.

These settings have a direct influence upon the student's openness to learning as well as to the way he will respond. Each student comes with some idea of "education" and what that idea is will make a great difference in his readiness to learn and in what he appropriates. It is a filter through which all future educational experiences will be screened.

In addition, the settings indicate the pressures upon the educational system of a society. In some instances formal education for children and youth reflects the expectations of power groups within the society. The claims of industry or government, or the demands of deprived ghetto dwellers, are part of the setting and constitute the conditions and limitations under which the educational system has to operate.

The patterns of education then become additional elements in the setting of the student. "Education" implies a conscious, intentional initiation of a process aimed at stimulating a particular type of learning. Whatever that process is, it becomes itself a selected setting from among many possibilities, and the setting will influence the education that takes place. The exterior setting of education—whether formal or informal—includes the factors of location, facilities, scheduling, procedures, grouping, subject matter, requirements, discipline, personal relationships, and organization.

All the elements of the setting are also elements of the content of the activity. Environment, content, and method are not three separate aspects. There may be a particular discrete subject matter, but what is presented about the subject matter, the environment in which the activity is conducted, and the processes employed in presentation are all parts of the content of the educational experience.

Those who "intend" to engage in education have a great variety of exterior settings within which to carry on such activities, whether in casual one-to-one encounters or in highly organized formal groups. The setting may be austere or comfortable, demanding or encouraging. The most obvious settings for children are home, community, school, and voluntary organizations, such as churches or clubs. For most people engaged in education—older youth and adults—the exterior setting may be university, institute, office, factory, or farm. Most "education" is carried on outside of "schools" and is seldom even called "education." When an employer plans an activity by which his employee may learn about the company or his own job, with freedom to respond, that is education. So the setting may be practically anywhere. When a setting is consciously arranged, the question to be raised of educators is whether or not the chosen setting is conducive to learning by *this* student. Since no a priori answer can be given to such a question, it becomes one of the basic responsibilities of a teacher to determine the answer in each situation.[33]

Chapter III

CULTURE

EDUCATION, of some sort, is an aspect of every culture. Every pattern of education, every philosophy of education, and every educational institution is both conditioned by its cultural setting and is an expression of that culture. One responsibility of an educator who tries to be self-conscious about his work is to identify the intended relationship between educational activities and the surrounding culture.[34] If the intention is only to reflect the culture, the educator is not under much critical strain.[35] However, if the intention of the educational activity is to enable students to evaluate or criticize or change their culture, the educator is pressed to develop a more substantial basis for what he does.

FUNCTIONS

The place of education within a culture may be described in functional terms. "Function" in cultural analysis refers to the interrelationship of elements within a culture.[36] Education, and particularly schools, within any society performs certain identifiable cultural functions. The most obvious is the contribution of education to cultural stability and perpetuation. By requiring each rising generation to be conditioned and indoctrinated by their elders in a consciously planned "educational" program, a society is helped to provide continuity.

At the same time education contributes to cultural change by consciously bringing members of the society into contact with ideas and persons which they would not meet without the intentional activity of others. Wherever thinking is required there is a threat to stability.

Educational patterns and institutions are expressions of particular groupings in a society, and thus of their subcultural standards. Those who are advantaged can participate in higher levels of educational opportunity, and as a result have even more advantage in sociocultural struggles. This tautology of the advantaged makes of the school an expression of cultural status.

As technical advances reduce working hours and increase leisure time in all societies, and thus reduce need for workers, schools perform a social function in keeping workers out of the labor market. In those professions requiring many years of preparation, the schools contribute even more to this delay. In schools large portions of the population are kept occupied in economically nonproductive activities, only part of whose function is to prepare students for later contributions to the society.

Education also provides outlets for benevolence. Though most education is supported out of public funds, still a very large proportion of education is privately supported. In the United States such benevolence is rewarded by reductions in income taxes, and by the status it provides for the givers.

Education provides encouragement and direction to national purposes and national goals. As such, education is an agent of the nation rather than an evaluator and critic of what the nation does.

The teaching of various disciplines which are concerned with aspects of culture, such as economics, music, history, physics, and psychology, may require quite different views of the relation of education to culture. A teacher of chemistry, for instance, may not be obliged to seek a perspective upon his cultural situation as would a teacher of history in order to perform competently. Still every educational program expresses sociological, historical, political, and economic views, just as it implies views of psychology and educational philosophy. And every educational program implies a particular interpretation of the total culture. Within the broad spectrum of disciplines it is the distinctive concern of cultural anthropology to attempt to describe patterns of inclusive relationships of the many aspects that constitute the whole culture. Because education is both a product and a reflection of its culture, cultural anthropology can be an important aid in understanding education, whether educational activities are directed toward perpetuating or changing their culture.

Anthropologists differ sharply among themselves over what culture is, and their diverse theories lead them to observe different things and offer differing explanations of what they see. Some anthropologists view culture as a set of materials and patterns existing in a community. Others view culture as some kind of cognitive system that gives meaning to the cultural phenomena.[37] Each approach has distinctive methods for analysis, description, and classification. Thus the relation of education to culture will differ according to whether one views it in terms of the first or the second of these views.

Within each of these major points of view there are a number of discrete theories, which in itself tends to suggest that the compilation of facts about materials and patterns is insufficient to explain the integrity of a culture. Culture is such an inclusive concept, and an analysis of a culture must deal with such a vast range of phenomena, that what one will see depends upon the theory from which it is viewed. Anthropology, like history, is a perspectivistic discipline.[38]

In either case, education is intimately related to culture. From the perspective of the first view, education is itself a set of materials and patterns within the larger cultural frame. From the perspective of the second it is a major means by which different cognitive systems are formed, examined, and revised. The relation of culture to education, therefore, needs to be examined from both points of view.

In every definition of culture there are four basic elements:

1. Culture connotes a total, inclusive pattern that relates many diverse elements into some kind of whole. The study of culture is, therefore, a holistic discipline.

2. Culture also connotes a discrete body of phenomena, so that it is possible to differentiate between an Incan culture and an Australian aboriginal culture.

3. Culture connotes a perspective from which to view the world—a world view—which both informs and directs the various elements of the culture.

4. And culture connotes material to which individuals and groups respond in acting and thinking.

Each of these has distinctive educational significance. Whatever varied ideas and activities education may deal with, they are related to a larger whole. It is not possible to consider any subject, event, or group in isolation from a larger cultural context. At the same time, the cultural setting of a student describes the limitation upon possibilities for patterns of action and types of world view within which he is able to act or think. The world view, however, provides direction as well as limitation. This tends to provide a common meaning for existence and thus the frame for resolving issues about what shall and shall not be done in meeting challenges of existence.

Contemporary world developments have raised a basic question for anthropology, Is it possible any longer to think in terms of discrete cultures? Are not all cultures now so pressed by cross-cultural contacts that the only adequate perspective is that of an emerging world culture? If so, education, in its preoccupation with the future, will need more and more to see its responsibilities in terms of understanding and implementing that emerging culture. The communications media, particularly of the more technically advanced countries, and the expansion of travel and trade continue to amplify the contacts and mutual influences of various cultures; and the rate of mutual influence increases with the speed of travel and communications.

Under these circumstances what were formerly called cultures may, perhaps, now be called subcultures. Even the large units of "civilizations" can be understood only as parts of a larger totality—the world setting in which all men live. Care must be taken, in speaking of a world "culture," not to use culture in a pejorative sense, nor to make more claims for unity than are justified. The diversity of cultures on the world scale is obvious, but the diversity within each culture is also very great. The perspective of cross-cultural contacts offers a distinctive contribution to the understanding of a society and of its education.[39]

ANTHROPOLOGY

Education and anthropology are related in many ways.[40]

1. Anthropology is part of education when it is an academic subject along with other academic disciplines.

2. Anthropology is used in education to study the cultural settings within which education is conducted, and for analyzing the influence of those settings upon educational processes.

3. Every educational program expresses some cultural patterns. Anthropology assists in analyzing the "culture of education."

4. Educational theory is influenced by its cultural setting, and anthropology serves education in helping to analyze both the roots of educational theory and its expression in particular theories.

5. Finally, anthropology is related to education at the level of relating anthropological theory to educational theory.

Inherent in all significant education is the capacity, the drive, to transcend its own cultural setting and bring a larger perspective to bear. It is at this point that the study of various cultures, which is the concern of anthropology, can be most helpful to education, because it offers one kind of perspective upon educational theory and practice. That perspective provides comparison—with other cultural patterns and views, and a basis for analyzing cultural diversity and unity. In this way anthropology helps education, of whatever kind, understand itself.

Anthropology is a descriptive and analytical discipline that reminds education that the adequacy of any educational venture depends, in the first place, upon the adequacy of its analysis of its situation. The anthropologist is concerned to look at the whole of a culture and thus is sensitive to the interrelationship and interaction of all aspects of the culture which might influence educational thinking and practice. Educational programs always imply an interpretation of the situation of the learners, so conscientious educators realize that they need to understand that situation if their programs are to be relevant.

An area of particular interest in educational-anthropological study is that of cross-cultural contacts. While the tools are not at hand to study with equal validity the educational patterns of all cultures, there is sufficient evidence to suggest that the advancement of education is directly related to the possibilities of cross-cultural contacts within a society. The areas of the world that have been the "crossroads" of history have usually enjoyed the highest cultural developments. These have been in different areas at different periods of history, but whether the points of intersection were the Middle East, Rome, London, or the Hanseatic cities, education was always more advanced at these centers than at the edges of areas of commerce. There were, of course, very practical reasons for pressure upon education. Language differences required someone who could interpret. Commerce required someone to keep records. The introduction of new products and new technologies threatened old ways of doing things. In the ferment at the intersection ideas and practices were challenged and either had to change or become revalidated. This was a direct stimulant to basic re-education.

Now that every part of the world is exposed to somewhat the same cultural interaction the world may be entering a new era of great stimulation and challenge for education. Since the present external setting of present-day education is total world exposure, an adequate educational theory needs to provide an understanding of how to handle the interaction of such diverse standards and patterns.[41]

Like anthropology, education is not an isolated discipline. It calls on many others for analyzing its situation, designing patterns, and conducting its activities. Like anthropology it is perspectivistic, and the adequacy of its perspective largely determines the adequacy of its programs. Repeatedly, new data calls for new interpretations and methods.

Chapter IV

INSTITUTIONS

A SCHOOL is an institution that draws students, for a time, into a special community, separate from the general community, where the educational process is formalized. Since educational activities, both informal and formal, may be conducted in the general community, placing students in a special community indicates an intention to have them learn something different from what they would learn from the community at large. A closed, traditional society does not need schools to initiate children into its traditions of behavior, belief, or skills. Yet if in such a society there is a special class, such as priests or folk doctors, which needs special knowledge that is kept from the general population, then the transmission of such knowledge usually requires a school. Or if a power group seeks to change the society's traditional patterns, then a separate special community provides the setting in which children may be initiated into ways of thinking and acting different from those of the population at large. On the other hand, in an open society where all citizens are exposed to diverse points of view and patterns of conduct, schools are not needed to stimulate change. The separate community, in such a society, tends to act as a brake upon change.

Schools are inherently conservative in relation to the particular objective that prompted their establishment. Whether the school is established to propagate the ideas of a great leader, or to implement a particular philosophy of education, or to form students for a particular kind of social behavior, the way it is organized tends to control its future development. Structures of authority, processes of decision-making, staffing procedures, expectations of constituents, all press the institution into a conserving function. The establishment of a school expresses an intention by some elements within a society to propagate skills, behavior, or beliefs, whether radical or traditional, that are different from those of the society as a whole; yet the separate, special community promptly develops its own conservative characteristics and vested interests, which limit its usefulness as an agent for social change. Even though the formalization of education into a school program tends to frustrate the intentions of its sponsors, there is great social pressure in most societies to measure education by the quantity of schooling.

Education as a social process usually becomes institutionalized.[42] To most people "education" means "schools," though it is difficult to reverse the definition and define education in such a way that it would include all the activities carried on by schools. Whatever its educational commitments may be, an institution develops a set of requirements for its own existence which may or may not coincide with its educational purpose.

Innumerable educational institutions are scattered across the landscape of the world, and their number increases daily with the growth of population, the development of "underdeveloped" regions of the earth, the proliferation of technical and academic specialization, and the constant hope of mankind that more and better education might correct its ills and save it from disaster.

These institutions come with a great profusion of characteristics which challenge categorization, because each institution takes on a "personality" as its various characteristics interact with one another. Yet it is possible to identify various "institutional designs" and to chart the implications of an institution's design for the effectiveness of each factor.

Usually "type" when applied to an educational institution is a very loose term referring to only one factor in the institution's design. By type may be meant graduate rather than undergraduate, or theological seminary rather than law school, or public school rather than private, or university rather than college. One factor does not give sufficient discrimination to discern the significance of different types, for in reality the variety may be very great among any one-factor type.

BASIC DISTINCTIONS

Formal or Informal. It may seem to be a contradiction in terms to speak of an informal institution, yet there are many significant educational programs conducted by loose associations of individuals or agencies. Conferences, consultations, institutes, conventions would be included in this category. In some instances this category would include programs that are incidental, or tangential, to other more formally organized activities, such as the retraining of mechanics which may result from the process of promoting the sale of a machine, or the education derived from the regular monthly meeting of the board of directors of a company or of the farm bureau.

Apprenticeship is an informal "institutionalized" type of education in many fields and in many parts of the world where traditional guild patterns still dominate in an occupation. While advanced work in such fields as farming, construction, and business administration may require university or graduate education, less demanding levels of these fields may depend totally on apprenticeship for the preparation of workers. In many religious groups, ministerial leadership is produced by an apprenticeship system rather than through academic theological institutions. Still, most schools are formally organized.

Public or Private. A major distinction in some countries is between public and private schools, though the terms may have differing meanings, for instance, in England where the "public" schools are privately supported. In some countries "public" means open to the public even though supported and controlled by nongovernmental groups. In the United States "public" means state-controlled and tax-supported. The schools may be on any level from nursery to advanced graduate work. Private schools, of whichever level, may include a wide range of commercial, industrial, and professional educational programs quite different from those of public institutions.

Institutions primarily devoted to academic education are concerned with understanding subject matter, while those primarily devoted to vocational education are concerned with developing occupational skills. The former may include private and public schools, both religious and secular, while the latter may include schools of art, music, dance, banking, bartending, medicine, agriculture, and all programs for trades.

In some countries a distinction must be made between religious and secular institutions of education. Both terms are subject to many variations and different interpretations. A religious school might be owned or sponsored by some church or sectarian group, or it may be state-supported and conducted by religious groups, or it may be privately or publicly supported and operated by laymen with a religious orientation. Monastic schools and theological seminaries would come within this category, though the religion or theology department of a state university may be considered a secular institution. Generally, by secular is meant institutions not controlled by religious bodies, though a number of colleges and universities clearly under the sponsorship or control of religious groups see themselves as secular. Only in the extremes of either category is the distinction between religious and secular sharp and clear. The lack of clarity in many instances only heightens the ambiguity of the church-state issue in education.

The support and control of educational institutions may be of several types:

Government-supported. Schools maintained by grants from central government agencies or by state approval of taxation for schools within the governmental unit, with centralized bureaucracy for operation or by leaving this to local boards and administrators.

Privately endowed. Schools controlled by a board of trustees or directors, where the faculty are employees. Many privately endowed institutions also receive government funds and charge fees.

Controlled by parent institution. Schools conducted by other institutions, such as an industry, or a particular company, a church, or a club, where control is in the parent institution rather than in the educational institution as such.

Self-supporting. Schools maintained by income from fees. Some may have a board of directors and others are run by the faculty. In a few instances they are run by students who employ faculty, and in some cases they are profit-making institutions and are called proprietary schools.

While the educational philosophy to which individuals in these four types of schools may be the same, it will inevitably be expressed differently according to the pressures of other considerations—funds available, expectations of sponsoring bodies, the philosophical commitments of trustees and faculty, etc.

Inclusive or Specialized. Public education, particularly at the primary and secondary levels, usually includes a wide variety of studies and activities, as do many colleges. A university is, by definition, an institution that includes a number of colleges and is devoted to the study of many subjects. Inclusive institutions, whether public or private, religious or secular, vary in the degree to which they attempt to integrate the diverse elements in their educational programs.

There is a tremendous range of specialized educational institutions, some of which are academic and others vocational. Obviously these are not mutually exclusive emphases, for every vocation involves some academic subject matter in its study, and it is equally difficult to imagine an academic subject with no vocational implications, even if it is only preparation for teaching that subject. The types of specialized institutions may be public or private, ranging from a one-month secretarial course to an advanced medical institute specializing in a particular disease.

Inclusive or specialized often involves the distinctions of size. A college may have 5,000 students, but if so, its activities are probably broadly inclusive. Universities with 40,000 or 50,000 students of necessity become different kinds of institutions, because of their size, from small liberal arts colleges. Size requires a different physical plant, economic structure, organizational pattern, type of faculty, relation to governmental units, relation to alumni, and all these profoundly influence the institution's academic program.

Media. The fourth basic distinction in type of educational institution is based upon the medium employed.

Most schools are built around classroom, textbook, and teacher. In some instances the classroom may be a field or workshop, and there may be material or lectures rather than textbooks, but this type provides the greatest measure of structural control and the employment of traditional media.

Increasing emphasis is being placed on education via mass media of movies, radio, television, newspapers, magazines, and books. If education can be defined as the presentation of material regardless of the response of "students," then the mass media are educational, though they may also be considered as material that may be useful in educational programs. Thus the mass media, with no way to control differentiation of hearers or readers, may be accepted as institutions providing educational resource materials.

A special category of educational institutions are those offering correspondence courses. In these there may be a certain degree of adapting what is done to the situation of the student, but usually this is so slight that correspondence schools could be included with mass media as providing resource materials for possible educational use.

STRUCTURES

The structure of an educational institution is a complex of many dimensions, each of which requires specific decisions in the process of organization:

Originator. This could be a national legislature, a professional group, a church, an individual, with highly diverse motivations of idealism or practical need for skills, or social concern, or desire for profit, who initiates the idea of having an educational institution.

Sponsor. This may be an individual, a governmental unit, an independent corporation, an association, a group of faculty, a group of students. In most countries this sponsoring body would need some legal status, particularly if a graduate of the school is to receive a certificate or a degree on the basis of which he can get a job or be admitted to other schools.

Administration. Someone needs to set up and administer whatever program is developed by the institution. This may be simply one person, as in a small country school, or it can be a vast machine as in a large university, or the bureaucracy of a state, city, or national ministry of education.

Location. The educational activities need to be conducted in some location. This could be in a home, in a one-room school, in a grove of trees, or on a campus of buildings designed for highly articulated special functions. Many decisions are involved in selecting a site, deciding what is needed, raising money, constructing and maintaining facilities.

Equipment and Facilities. The physical accouterments of an educational institution may be as simple as a bench and a chalkboard, or they may be so complex that a staff is needed to administer the acquisition and maintenance of buildings, grounds, books, supplies, audio-visual equipment, laboratory tools, surgical instruments, animal feed, etc. An institution with residents will require many facilities not needed in other schools.

Teaching Staff. The range from simplicity to complexity is as great here as in the matters noted above. A school may have one teacher or thousands. There may be a few or many gradations of rank or salary. Arrangements for hiring may be a simple two-person agreement, or may be a long chain of committee approvals, board decisions, governmental clearance, negotiations with unions, etc. The maintenance of a faculty may involve tenure, leaves, advanced study, sabbaticals, and writing privileges.

Program. What is to be taught and how may be an obviously simple matter in a school of sculpture or hairdressing or auto mechanics. Yet in a high school of five thousand students or a large university the range of curricular requirements and patterns of teaching and study may be immense, calling for a great deal of administrative time to work out and keep the whole operating smoothly, requiring varied facilities and equipment and library resources.

Size. Varieties of number are limitless. There may be a million students in a single urban system, or five in a highly specialized college. Nevertheless, there will always need to be a procedure for recruiting, registering, and handling students in any institution. Increase in size tends to increase the need for organization and administration in geometric proportions.

Students. The most common identification of educational institutions is in reference to levels of academic advancement: primary, secondary, university, graduate, postgraduate. At the lower levels these are, in practice, synonymous with age levels, and at the higher levels there is a rough relation with age. In some instances the level is indicated by the degree given at the end of a program, but there can be great differences in the quality of work offered in schools claiming to be secondary or university or graduate. In many countries, of course, college refers to secondary school rather than to university level.

While many educational institutions are open to a general student clientele, others restrict the student body by sex, or age, or occupation, or race. The cost of private schools may automatically limit the student body to one social class, and entrance examinations may limit to one intellectual level.

The range of responsibility taken by an educational institution may vary greatly based on how much of the students' lives is to be cared for by the institution. Boarding schools

and resident colleges require very different institutional structures from day schools and commuter universities. Some
schools provide residence for faculty only, or for part of the
student body, and thus incorporate both types of institutional
structure.

Alumni Organization. Institutions that depend for income
upon former students, or that attempt to function as continuing
education of those who participated in basic orientation to the
field in that institution, may develop elaborate agencies for
keeping contact, distributing material, and raising money
among alumni.

Special Services. A university may produce community studies or do military research on contract. A medical school may
conduct a hospital; a school of social work may conduct a
settlement house; or a school of education may conduct a demonstration nursery. Many universities, colleges, seminaries, and
technical schools produce books, professional or technical
journals. Many schools operate commercial establishments
such as department stores, apartment buildings, television or
radio stations, dairies, bookstores, farms, and barber shops.

SOCIAL FUNCTIONS

Institutions perform a variety of social functions in every
culture.[43] The conscious rationale for most institutions is that
they provide the facility for social cohesion and cooperation.
The particular patterns employed may vary with the type of
concern that inspires common effort, or the type of product
that requires cooperative action. But beyond these rather obvious uses of the machinery of institutions there are more crucial functions that have important consequences for a culture.

Institutions are instruments for maintaining the *status quo.*
The processes by which institutions are formed inevitably establish the present and limit the future. Even those institutions
devoted to encouraging innovation or social change bear

within their structures and ideology the situation that gave them birth, and they cannot escape their generation. Thus institutionalism is a social process for self-perpetuation. When a club elects officers it does so by procedures considered normative at the time, and even without a "constitution" the procedure becomes precedent. When that same club adopts a constitution it is saying, in effect, that all future members must act in keeping with the founders' views of proper procedure. When an industry or a political party or a group of insurgents or a tribal council organizes itself, it institutionalizes its patterns of action as a protection against an uncertain future. Changes will come but the function of institutions is to delay or channel the changes.

An even more important function of institutions is to legitimize collective action and protect decision makers. This makes it possible, in the inevitable conflicts in a society, to divert substantive issues into procedural questions. The processes of interrelationship become the prior concerns of institutionalized life, and participants are saved from the anxiety of responsibility if they can be assured that their actions are appropriate within the legitimized procedures of the institution. Innovation, then, must find some rationalization within the bounds of legitimacy in order to be acceptable. When there is ardent loyalty to the details of institutional structure, or to its originally stated purpose, or to its particular processes, the possibilities of innovation are severely limited; the claims of legitimacy become a kind of "morphological fundamentalism."

In all these ways institutions perform a stabilizing function in society. They stand against the dynamics of history by attempting to preserve the past, or they promote certain types of social change that express the interpretation of history of their initiators and usually fail to anticipate subsequent historical developments. Though the function of educational institutions is often assumed to be anticipation of the future, most societies employ such institutions to conserve prior values or to attempt to channel social change in preferred directions.

INSTITUTIONAL DYNAMICS[44]

Within each of the categories noted above there are many kinds of institutions. They are classed together because of their preoccupation with education, regardless of their motivation or the quality of program they conduct. They are distinguished from other institutions—industrial, religious, governmental—by their distinctive concern, yet there is a constant interaction among these various types of institutions so that the shape of each may be less than distinct. The processes, too, are very similar.[45]

Public schools are organized in much the same way as a business; the educational bureaucracies of churches are very similar to the bureaucracies of state boards of education. Yet mixed with these modern parallels are long traditions carried down from the medieval period in guilds, colleges, and universities.[46]

Each culture tends to have its own distinctive patterns of institutional modes. In some cultures each institution is an extended family, and institutional practices are determined by their impact on family relationships. In other cultures institutions are impersonal. Some institutions are primarily politically oriented, while others are primarily technical. Some institutions are the reflection of an individual personality, with all significant control in his hands, while in others personal influence is reduced to a minimum and "the committee" is in charge.

Educational institutions do not produce an "end product" except, perhaps, the books and magazines published by a university press. Seldom are they able to claim exclusive influence upon people who have participated in their programs. The contribution of a school to its graduates is very difficult to measure. For this reason schools are subjected to many pressures that cannot be registered by objective measurements of contribution. Prestige, in the eyes of the public and within the guild of a profession, is the objective of educational institutions dependent upon benevolence or governmental grants. Prestige helps build faculties and draw students, yet the search for prestige may subject a school to public pressures that might undercut prestige. In educational institutions within an industry, or in public schools where attendance is required, public opinion is less important. Nevertheless, one of the powerful forces shaping most educational institutions is the pressure of expectation on the part of sponsors, teachers, students, the public, and agencies waiting to employ graduates. Where democratic decisions can determine school policy and program these "expectations" lead the school into many activities which may have little or no relation to education itself. In the United States both public schools and universities have been largely defenseless against such escalating expectations. Schools have amplified programs and are pressed to perform such a wide range of public services that education often has to take its place behind sports, health services, community projects, etc.

So both in patterns of organization and types of program schools are shaped by the society in which they are set. But sometimes they are also shaped by creative response to obvious need and the attraction of patterns encountered from other cultures. The American college was copied from the colleges of Cambridge and Oxford. The rise of "progressive education" in the United States was a direct result of the spread of child psychology and new patterns of education from such Europeans as Rousseau, Pestalozzi, and Froebel. Around the world in mid-twentieth century there is a very busy trade in educational ideas. Perhaps the heaviest currents are from "developed" to "developing" nations, but as exporters of educational ideas must realize if they are honest, all creativity is not to be found in the United States and Europe. Patterns employed in these countries may not necessarily be best for others, in fact they may be dangerous in other cultural settings.[47]

The term "institution" is used here in reference to consciously organized social structures designed to facilitate common action.[48] An "institution" may be a rural cooperative, a

national army, a church, a grocery store, an automobile manufacturer, or the United Nations. Many educational agencies
are institutions, though education is not limited to the activities
of such institutions. However, the institutionalization of educational activities introduces into those activities a set of factors
that derive from "the natural history" or "the logic of institutional life."

Organization, and the resulting institutions, is necessary to
social life. Men must work together to derive the benefits of the
earth, to satisfy bodily and aesthetic needs, and to maintain
social order. They must work together to confirm their humanity. Human cooperation has taken an infinite variety of forms,
some of which are typical of a particular culture and others
which are transcultural. Institutions are continuously in the
process of change and adaptation to their *cultural shape*. The
birth of an institution usually is the result of a felt need or want
combined with initiative among those willing to organize
to meet the need. The pattern of organization may be creative
and distinctively adapted to the particular situation and need,
or it may be traditional. In Western culture the form taken by
an organization is often quite automatic: set up a committee;
select chairman, secretary, and treasurer; write a constitution;
elect a board of trustees; form a corporation; meet monthly;
operate by Robert's Rules of Order; keep minutes; hold elec-
tions annually for specified terms of office; have a publication
for all members; hold an annual budget drive (if it is a voluntary organization); prepare annual reports and approval of
budget; select a staff; and build a building. This pattern of
organization is virtually automatic because the people involved
assume that "everyone organizes this way." By mutual agreement the wheels of social cooperation are greased, there are
mechanisms for resolving differences of implementing consensus and channeling (or removing the threat of) creativity, as
well as for assuring participants that what is being done is
legitimate and reliable.

Described in this way the institution may seem to be impersonal, but no institution would operate smoothly for any length of time if it were not personalized. Efficient social cooperation depends upon the morale of those who participate as well as upon the structure of the organization. To express it in reverse, a very crude organization may produce valuable results when morale is high, and a very sophisticated organization may be very inefficient because of low morale. However, there are limits to what even the highest morale may produce.

One of the elements in morale is *loyalty*. Every organization requires a measure of loyalty, that is, of personal commitment to the objectives and the procedures of the organization. Those in leadership positions personify the institution, and loyalty to the institution may become synonymous with loyalty to the leadership. At times of conflict over possible actions of the organization, however, appeals are often made by both sides to be loyal to the institution and its purposes rather than to the persons who happen to be leaders at the present time. Outside the organization—whether government, business, school, or church—the leader or top executive usually personifies the institution. The extent to which this is justified usually depends upon the point of view of the leader. If he sees himself as an enabler of democratic action and decentralized responsibility, he may personify its processes but not the direction and dynamic of the institution. On the other hand, if the executive insists on holding all decision-making in his own hands, he may personify both the power and the weakness of the institution.

Loyalty is only one of the claims made by institutions upon those working within them or served by them. Participants in the life of an organization are expected to commit themselves to its purpose and goal, and this is usually expressed in mythical terms as a description of its origins. The present organization is expected to "remain true" to the *image of the purpose* which led to its founding. Business institutions are freer from this pressure than others because if a firm started by trading in hides and now makes automobiles, this can be justified by pointing to the record of profits, for profit is a goal or purpose to which most businesses in capitalist countries must be faithful. Service organizations, clubs, churches, and schools, are all institutions that try to keep vivid in the minds of participants the origin and purposes of the organization, and as circumstances change the interpretations change, so what is presented is usually a symbolic view. However it is described, every institution must have an accepted "purpose," which provides cement for keeping the participants working together in common loyalty. While each worker or member may have his own interpretation of that reason for being, in addition there is usually a publicly expressed or assumed purpose ascribed to the institution which tends to govern its relationships with other people or other institutions. Thus loyalty and devotion are not only to its present existence but also to its historic significance and original intent.

However, the dynamics of the institution cannot be controlled by devotion to myths about its origin and purpose, for circumstances cannot stand still, and as they change, the institution is seldom able to change accordingly, so that increasingly the purpose shifts to the preservation of the institution itself.[49] The institution becomes its own self-justification.[50] People come to depend upon it for livelihood and the society at large comes to expect its continuation.[51] When the original explicit intent becomes too irrelevant the institution is forced to find new purposes to justify its continued existence. These are usually provided by the incidental purposes that have coalesced around the central ones. Thus it is that secondary values become primary, even though the structure of the institution was not designed to perform these activities effectively.

Since institutions are organized to provide machinery for social activity, they are essentially tools for relationships between persons and groups in common activities, whether commercial, political, religious, or educational. Whatever the general type, every institution is a *political construct*. Whatever the type of culture or society in which it exists, so long as it requires persons to agree, combine efforts, relate, work together, etc., some machinery must be developed to win or force such unity of effort. Politics is the art of converging social effort so that something can be done together. A common negative attitude toward politics only means that many people refuse to admit the political character of their institutions. This is dangerous because it leads to actions decided upon without taking all relevant circumstances into account. In reality it is impossible to have a nonpolitical institution. Whether the need is for stability or for change, ways must be worked out for decision-making by someone, and for the decisions to reflect enough consensus so that the organization can operate with at least minimal efficiency.

The presence or absence of *competition* may make a great difference in the mode of an institution's operation. If there is only one church or only one school in a community, and only one paper manufacturer or one bus line in a country, the tensions over what is to be done and how will be within that one institution. If, on the other hand, there are many churches and schools, and several paper manufacturers and bus lines, the economic and political situation is more complex. Competition between institutions may make each more efficient or, as often happens, it may lead to institutional imperialism in which each tries to outdo the other in enlarging services or activities. Each institution, in other words, must continue to justify its existence in the light of the expectations of the external setting within which it operates.

In some cases this leads institutions to regular reevaluation of their activities and effectiveness. Since monopoly is always difficult to maintain against creative competition, the temptation to imperialism may be countered by a clarification of the distinctive function of each institution. Obviously distinctiveness is an interpretation by someone in the light of need and capacity. An electric power company may recognize the need for better wholesale vegetable markets in a region, but it does not have the capacity to meet that need, any more than a well-organized vegetable market could meet the need for electric power.

Each of the factors that provide dynamics for an institution —cultural shape, loyalty, images of origin and purpose, political construct, competition—may be subject to extensive variation and profoundly influence the institutional design. Each factor, as well as all of them when brought together into an institutional "personality," becomes subject to institutionalism.

EDUCATIONAL INSTITUTIONALISM

Whether nursery-kindergartens, correspondence schools, an art academy, or high schools and universities, all educational institutions are caught by the necessity of some pattern of organization and subsequently with the consequences of the pattern selected. Schools are conscious constructs of a society, and their pattern of organization is deeply influenced by the culture in which they are set. Schools, too, take on personality as reflected by teachers and administrators. To many children the "school" is the teacher.

Schools require the loyalty and devotion of administrators, teachers, students, and other related personnel if they are to be effective, but in most schools there is disagreement over the object of loyalty—traditions, patterns of operation, teaching methods, administrative leaders, favorite teachers, etc. Schools, too, ardently maintain myths about their origin and purpose, and loyalty is in part loyalty to those myths.[52] Schools have set up structures that are devoted to self-maintenance, regardless of the validity of the educational activity to which the institution was originally devoted. Around the central purposes have often grown many incidental activities which sometimes claim much greater attention and loyalty than the central function.

Educational institutions are arenas of political activity, whether nursery-kindergartens, a state board of education, a school of medicine, or an institute of technology. There are incessant pressures for change, both external and internal, and some machinery must be provided for resolving differences and obtaining some convergence of direction and effort. Administrators are not the only ones involved in the politics of an educational institution. Teachers and students, sponsors and clients, all figure in the pull and haul of ideas, the necessity of meeting criticism and resolving differences, as well as the need to maintain support.

Obviously there is political tension and pressure between educational institutions in any community or region or state. This conflict may be met by sharpening the distinctive focus of the institutions' programs or by an imperialistic spreading out into more activities and services on the part of each one.

These points of similarity between educational and other institutions are balanced by points of contrast. Educational institutions attempt to express a philosophy of education, and therefore of necessity are deductively initiated organizations. Since, as noted above, there is no way to make a definitive evaluation of the "product" of an educational institution, it is more clearly dependent upon measuring its effectiveness either by participation or by its apparent implementation of its philosophy. In the light of some interpretation of need, each type of educational institution tends to develop a distinctive type of philosophy, yet no philosophy can be directly institutionalized. When the attempt is made, certain "institutional necessities" intrude for which a philosophy of education usually has no particular concern. For instance, how many people should be on a board of directors, where should a school building be located, how many administrative staff personnel or how many secretaries should there be? Someone must make decisions about such matters, and hundreds more, when setting up an educational institution, so that philosophical commitments, political considerations, and economic necessities all qualify each other in the process of institutionalization. And as time goes on each continues to make its claim so that the educational needs of students or teachers are only two of many considerations which administrators must take into account in making any decision.

The necessity of vast economic commitments to maintain

schools, whether from government funds, school taxes, endowments, or contributions, means that educational institutions have to develop vast reservoirs of loyalty to the institution in order to assure future income. The loyal people who "pay" do not need to know anything about what is done in the institution except enough to keep paying, which may allow a gulf to develop between sponsors and supporters and can produce a situation of irresponsibility on the part of those who have power within the school.

The varieties and complexity of elements that make up the design of an educational institution help to explain the power of institutionalism in educational affairs. The more elaborate the enterprise the greater is the need for formalized structures. The more formalized the structure the greater is the inertia and resistance to change. There is no necessary relation between the changing situation in which a school is set and the changes within the institution. Unless there is a direct change of economic sources (and many institutions are able to insulate themselves against this by building up reserves or endowment) or a specific change in sponsorship, most educational institutions are left to change by the processes of internal politics or attrition.

It is also apparent that in larger and more formalized educational institutions the distinctly educational activities (teaching and learning) have a less and less important place. Fewer decisions in other aspects of institutional life are determined by their influence upon the specifically educational activities.

Also the larger and more formal the educational institution becomes the more differentiation of function among educators —leading to specialization and professionalization. Leaving aside the issue of whether education is a discipline or a profession, the thousands of persons engaged in "the profession of education" on its many levels in all countries of the world make professionalism and its attendant problems one of the major elements in educational institutionalism.[53]

There are so many possible institutional forms that educational activities could take that the relation of structure to program is always open-ended, and subject to the views of education held by those in decision-making positions in the educational system. But if a person is to understand the nature of contemporary education, he must recall that most people think of education as the activity of an institution, a school. He must also realize how complex are the elements that are involved in an educational institution and the various factors that lead to institutionalization. Only then can it become clear that the trust that many societies place in education is in reality trust placed in a *system*. The public relations of prestigious universities seek to equate attending that institution with getting a good education. But within the university is a system so elaborate and complex that it would never be possible to provide empirical proof that it produces a better educated person than some other university. Since such proof is not possible the principal motivation for attending must be faith in the structure, the system, and the processes carried on there. Thus can commitment to education become commitment to institutionalism.

Chapter V

PROCESSES

THE PROCESSES of education are usually assumed to be derived deductively from articulated objectives. Logical steps from philosophy to goal to process to classroom procedure seem to be obvious. However, no educator has the privilege of such a pristine approach. Everywhere in the world educational processes and institutions are already established and the only opportunity fresh philosophical or procedural ideas have is to modify patterns that have been employed for years or centuries.

Practice precedes philosophy. Obviously some philosophical point of view is implied in every educational procedure, but philosophizing about education is a reflective function—reflecting upon given patterns of social activity. Examinations of educational processes illuminate the struggles to clarify and articulate educational theories and objectives. This should be obvious because the structures and processes of this social activity derive their modes and models from other activities of the surrounding society.

Exploration of the relation between philosophy and practice must accept the fact that established processes have a powerful influence both upon the philosophy and upon the goal. Because processes are part of the content of every educational activity, they tend to be self-validating and self-perpetuating. Seldom are individual educators or groups able to "forget" the processes by which they were educated, so there is little possibility of their starting *de novo* in designing a set of processes. Even "utopias" reflect the patterns and structures of the society they would replace. Philosophies and goals do not lead, by simple deductive steps, to the processes and procedures of effective education. There is a reverse flow of factors which must be considered at each stage, so that the relation between philosophy and program moves continually in both directions.

A phenomenological analysis of education begins with the existing phenomena, which is a set of processes *within* which various philosophies, goals, and types of procedure are in constant interaction. The articulation, modification, and revision of philosophy, or the clarification of objectives, is part of one of the essential processes of education.

STAGES

There are three essential stages in the processes of education, each of which may be an elaborate and variegated set of activities; and each is dependent on the others. The first stage is that which deals with the structuring of the overall system. This is the *systemizing stage*, where the concern, if one is to be self-conscious about it, is with the whole system and how it will operate. The simplest apprenticeship may follow patterns and processes of training that have been established for centuries. Teaching a young Indian how to make a canoe follows a traditional system, which prescribes when such training begins, where it will be done, by whom, according to what procedures, how long it will take, and the testing of the results.

Similarly, a modern university requires a systemizing stage (though of far greater scope), which includes designing buildings, ordering supplies, hiring teachers, operating a bookstore, adopting statements of purpose, evaluating procedures, issuing schedules, collecting fees.

The processes within the systemizing stage may be very

informal or highly bureaucratized. In contemporary educational systems these processes borrow from, and depend upon, processes of many other fields such as investment counselors, computer analysts, psychological testing, plant management, and publication specialists.

Education is always a system, though it may be conducted in a very unsystematic way. The overall system may be so simple as a mother arranging the utensils in the kitchen in preparation for teaching her daughter how to bake a cake, or it may be so elaborate that it employs thousands of specialists in hundreds of fields, all backing up more thousands of teachers who work with millions of students. If the educational program of a nation, a province, a city, an industry, a family, a church, or a union is to be consciously planned and conducted, someone needs to be concerned with the processes by which the overall system is developed and operated. The system may be consciously planned or may be unthinkingly adopted from traditional use, but it is always present. Systemizing activities are designed to facilitate education, and are essential to an educational program, but they may not in themselves be educational; that is, they may not be conducted in such a way that they facilitate or encourage learning among participants of that stage.

A second stage of educational processes has to do with the activities of teachers, tutors, dons, or other persons in direct contact with learners, and may be designated the *pedagogic stage*. The "teacher," whoever this may be, is responsible for planning and conducting the processes of an educational occasion, whether it takes place among the birch trees where canoes are made, in a carpenter shop where a boy is apprenticed to a master carpenter, in the kitchen where a mother is teaching her daughter to bake, in an operating room where a surgeon is supervising an intern, or in the primary classroom of a public school. The activities of teachers may be formal or informal, may incorporate several methods or only one. They range from initial planning through presentation and evaluation. These activities often depend upon the subject matter: the teaching of canoe-making by apprenticeship would not ordinarily demand a wide variety of methods. On the other hand, the study of the social sciences, or music, or philosophy, or business administration may require many different methods to be effective. In such fields the basic teaching processes and methods to be used are subject to the professional judgment of the teacher and cannot be prescribed in advance without consideration of the learner and his situation.

The third stage of educational processes includes the activities of the learner, and may be designated as the *curricular stage*. "Curriculum" includes all the activities and materials initiated by the teacher for the student's use or participation. Implicit in the idea of curriculum is subject matter, its organization, its sequence in study on the one hand, and its adaptation to the situation of the learner on the other. Both teacher and learner participate in the choice of the curriculum, for what one student says may be the "content" of what others in the class will learn. But the effort to adapt subject matter to situation is a distinctive responsibility of teachers. Curriculum may include private study by prospective Chinese scholars in their individual examination booths in Peking, or the discussion of would-be philosophers in the Academy with Socrates; or it may include assigned reading in a library or the outline of themes to be discussed in a seminar; it may include the waiting for chemical reaction in a test tube or the practice sermons of a theolog.

SYSTEMIZATION

The pedagogic and curricular processes of an educational system may be seen in particularly close interaction in any educational occasion, so education is often seen as nothing more than teaching and learning. However, this is inadequate even on a very simple or primitive level, because a more inclusive system is always implicit in every educational occasion. On more advanced levels the preparatory processes may become so extensive that the processes of the educational occasion are submerged beneath the mounting levels of educational structures and agencies.

Some small or specialized schools may escape certain steps of the processes set up for larger schools, such as governmental approval, production of textbooks, films, supplies and equipment, and the preparation of teachers. However, the landscape of contemporary education in any country is covered by a variety of systems of processes now considered essential for good education. They are noted here in sequence from the most inclusive to the most particular.

Educational Agencies—national, regional, local. A wide range of associations, organizations, and movements are deeply concerned about, and have a considerable influence upon, all levels of education. This would include associations of schools, parent-teacher organizations, student movements, professional educational societies, and accreditation agencies. Some agencies are set up by vested interests to pressure school systems, while others are set up to raise money for particular kinds of schools. Foundations may come within this category when they develop programs specifically designed to influence school policies. Some educational bureaucracies, such as general church agencies, might be considered in this same category. All these agencies are engaged in many processes for determining position and influence of educational practices.

Levels of Control. In some countries every public school is controlled directly from a national ministry of education. In others this control may be decentralized. In the United States educational control, within limits of the national constitution, is vested in the states, which in turn authorize local boards of education to set up and conduct the schools. In both patterns there are extensive bureaucracies, each involving elaborate processes of decision-making, controls, accounting, relation to levels above and below, personnel, etc.

Resources and Materials. Every educational system requires many types of text and resource materials. In some countries these are officially produced by governmental agencies, while in others many private commercial concerns produce books, maps, supplies, furniture, and audio-visual equipment. Elaborate processes are required in each step of selecting and producing each type of material. This becomes most elaborate when materials must be officially approved.

Preparation of Personnel. Each school system requires personnel to conduct its administrative and teaching activities. In some societies the qualifications are determined by heredity or are passed on from generation to generation by apprenticeship, whereas in others there is an extensive formal process by which teachers and administrators are selected, trained, supervised, advanced, and maintained.

School Administration. School administrators have the specific responsibility of designing and executing the structures and procedures by which the school will be conducted. Whether simple or elaborate, the process is a distinct set that must take into account all pressures and expectations of groups inside and outside the school.

Teaching Processes[54]

A basic distinction needs to be recognized in the whole spectrum of processes of educational occasions between situations where work can be *required* for graduation, degrees, getting a job, advancement, grades, etc., and educational situations in which all work is *voluntary* without the pressure of degrees or grades or other extraneous considerations.

Required work points toward a two-step process—of presentation and testing. The presentation may be a lecture or an assignment, and the testing may be informal as discussion is carried on in class, or it may be formal in examinations or papers. The process of grading, also, may be simply a means for expressing the judgment of a teacher, or it can be by various objective levels in which grading is the function of an assistant, other students, or some other agency to which the school is related—as in the British university system where college examinations are graded and degrees issued by a related university. In a situation of required work the motivation and interest of the student are of little concern to the system (though it may be of concern to the teacher, and may influence the quality of work the student does). If the school is preparing skilled technicians or professionals with precise competencies, the qualifications for graduation and degree may be quite objective and must be met regardless of the personal factors involved. On the other hand, if the qualifications are those set by the school to maintain its own views of high standards, the pressures upon the student may depend more upon his own motivation, and the judgment of competency may be much more subjective on the part of the teacher. Therefore different sets of processes may appropriately be employed in these types of educational situations.

When the work is voluntary, the teacher may take a detached stance and respond to the initiative of students or may accept responsibility for eliciting and encouraging participation. In most adult education programs participation is voluntary, and the incentive of students is not based on the need for grades and degrees. If the teacher needs only to respond to the interest of students, he is free to use a much wider range of teaching and study processes than when he must entice students to come and to remain. Developing interest may be quite different from directing interest which is already there.

If the work is voluntary and interest needs to be developed, processes for eliciting interest would be closely related to the reason the student comes at all. Is he there because parents require it, or because of the status he might derive from participation, or to meet his girl friend? In voluntary associations that conduct educational activities, such as churches and clubs, attendance is pressed as a matter of loyalty. Obviously a teacher or an administrator must take these into account in deciding which methods would be most likely to encourage interest.

As noted above, the processes of an educational occasion form a bridge between the claims of the subject matter and the situation of the student. Some of the processes are inherent in the structure of the institution and the teacher has little control over them, while others are so subject-dominated that there is very limited opportunity for the teacher to adjust to the concerns and interests of the students. The more personal the subject matter the more it depends upon the interpretation and appropriation of the student, and the greater the freedom of the teacher in adapting and revising methods of classroom procedure. However, the availability of materials and equipment also are limiting factors that must be taken into account. It is difficult to teach a medical student how to diagnose measles when no one around has measles, just as it is difficult to teach astronomy without a telescope.

Behind the details of any educational occasion are several basic processes that are equations of the relation of matter, teacher, and student. The types described below are not necessarily coterminal with particular methodologies. Each refers to a discrete set of relationships and direction of activity among the three elements—teacher, matter, student. Each of these can be diagramed: T for teacher, M for matter, and S for student or students; the line enclosing each diagram suggesting that each process is always conducted in a particular (internal-external) setting that qualifies the process; and the arrow indicating the movement of the process in each instance.

Distributive. This process is one of action directed by the teacher toward students with the teacher in control of the entire process. The teacher is the authority and "distributes" his knowledge or theory or expertise directly to students with no pro-

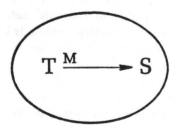

vision for determining their response. The movement is from teacher to student.

Directive. When a teacher draws upon a body of knowledge or the authority of another person in order to enlighten students the basic process is a directive one. The distinction between this and the distributive process is that the teacher draws upon

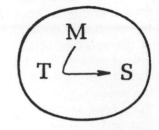

ideas, data, theories, or interpretations other than his own, and directs them toward students. This is similar to the distributive process in that no provision is made, within the process, for tracing the response of students.

Indicative. When a teacher points students to authorities outside himself, when he arranges for them to encounter the material, when he challenges them to look at what he is looking at, then he has initiated the indicative process. As in the two

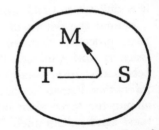

prior processes, he does not attempt to control the students' response, but his influence is exercised in the selection of what he suggests that they examine.

Reactive. When the teacher responds to students' activities, then a reactive process is taking place. Usually this involves the discussion method, but it may also include evaluation of individual work, comments on an examination paper, or even the

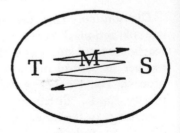

more indirect planning of program in the light of some identification of student situation or need. The reactive process can
include challenging and questioning both by the teacher and
by students.

Redirective. When a teacher
enables the students in the class
to engage in mutual challenge,
encounter, confrontation, questioning, demonstration, discussion, etc., this is evidence of a
redirective process. In this the
teacher may stand aside and only

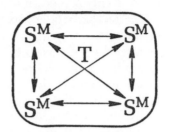

encourage the encounter taking place without engaging on
his own.

Demonstrative. A teacher may
perform the act that a student is
to learn to perform, or may set
up a procedure designed to illustrate a principle, or organize a
class as a case study—and these
would be expressions of the demonstrative process. The teacher

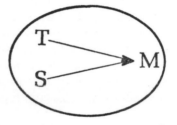

and student stand side by side in studying a matter, each
contributing to the other. The demonstration may be related
to another process, or it may be employed alone. In itself the
demonstrative process, like the distributive and indicative,
exercises no control over the student's response or appropriation.

Within each of these processes it is possible to manipulate
and condition students. Whether this is done is determined
by the teacher's own convictions about the appropriate function of education. In some ranges of learning, particularly
those dealing with technical matters, when precise skills are
needed (for instance, in mathematics, surgery, or chemistry,

etc.) students must develop skill or dexterity in certain manipulative activities in order to employ them in their fields. Indoctrination is essentially a manipulative process when it allows only one possible "answer" to the matter being considered, offering only one possible response from students.

The teacher who wants to escape involvement with the life or thought or experience of students will concentrate on the manipulative use of these processes. He may develop them into a fine skill, may be able to display brilliant pyrotechnics in lectures and in the question and answer periods following, but this can be the limit of his concern. The first three processes —distributive, directive, and indicative—all can be employed in this way by the teacher who does not want to get involved. They are essentially teacher-oriented and unless occasion is found to discover and take into account what is happening in the students in response to what is being done, their use can stand in the way of significant learning taking place. While no teacher can control what happens in a student, the teacher's concern to adapt what he does to the student's situation is a reflection of the teacher's view of his role.

The reactive and redirective processes are more clearly student-oriented, though they both provide ample opportunity for the teacher to bring his insight and understanding to bear in the educational situation. Both can be employed in a manipulative manner if the teacher is clever and does not wish to allow students to make their own interpretations of what takes place. These processes, including the use of the indicative when it is in response to student understanding, can be inductive when employed with openness to student ideas and experiences.

Most good teachers employ all six processes so that the pattern of teaching is determined by the "mix" of various processes. This mix expresses the teacher's philosophy of education and the care with which he is attempting to express it in this particular educational situation. The teacher who believes that education should be essentially transmission will usually employ the distributive and directive processes. The teacher who believes that education must allow freedom for the student to choose his own response to the experience will employ the redirective, demonstrative, and reactive processes more frequently.

The choice of one or another process is the responsibility of a teacher, and its place in the whole program of a school is the responsibility of an educator. Since there is no way to specify in advance what would be the appropriate methods to employ with a student or a class, it is necessary that someone appraise the situation and make the choice in the light of that situation. And since the situation changes continually that responsibility is a continuous one. Furthermore, the analysis needs to be made by someone near enough to be able to discern all relevant factors, which usually means the person who is in direct contact with the students, that is, the teacher.

Of course there are many sources of information that the teacher can take into account in appraisal: the personal response of the student, his verbalization about his situation, the records of prior accomplishments, his relation to others in the class, his capacities in dealing with subject matter, the interpretation of others who know him—parents, friends, classmates —as well as the elements of the larger external setting shared by both teacher and student. Putting these all together into a shaped interpretation of a particular student can seldom be done formally or systematically but most teachers do it nonetheless. They may seldom have occasion to articulate that appraisal, and when asked to do so often demur, but still they act toward each student in terms of some implicit interpretation of who he is and what his situation is, which may be no more than the teacher's imaginary projection of the world of the student.[55] Acting upon such an appraisal, choosing what shall be done with a class without consciously identifying and examining one's own motives in appraisal, is irresponsibility. Undoubtedly many good teachers have a "feel" or "sense" of the situation, but operating only on that feel is insufficient for responsible teaching, for only by consciously checking over all possible sources of insight and information can a teacher be certain that he has taken into account all that should be considered in planning the processes of an educational occasion.

Perhaps the distinguishing mark of the teacher is his recognition that the learner has a claim upon him.[56] There can be no realistic teaching that does not respond to that claim of the learner for the teacher to appreciate the setting from which he comes, to speak within his range of linguistic ability, to explain matters being discussed in terms of his intellectual level, and to deal with the immediate object of study in terms of his stage of comprehension.

Having taken all factors of the student's situation into consideration, a teacher decides on basic processes and the methods to express them in keeping with his view of their appropriateness in the particular circumstances, and his judgment of what is appropriate is an expression of three interrelated factors:

his philosophy of education,

his understanding of his competency with methods, and

his appraisal of the student's capacity for appropriation. These apply whether the teacher is engaged in group or in individualized instruction.[57]

Each educational occasion provides a feedback to the teacher which tests each of the above factors. It may provide the occasion for questioning the validity of his philosophy. It may cause the teacher to revise his judgment of his own methodological skill. The occasion may give him reason to change his interpretation of what the student may or may not comprehend. If the teacher is open to this feedback, it will then influence his decision about what processes and methods to employ on the next occasion. Above all it may demonstrate that the teacher has misinterpreted the situation of the student, and new elements must be taken into account. On the other hand, the occasion may confirm to the teacher the adequacy of his philosophy, his methodology, his expectations of the student, and his original appraisal of the student's situation.

This set of activities on the part of the teacher is but one segment of a larger set of processes which include the structure of the institution and its relation to regional and national organizations. The educator is one who performs each particular task in conscious relation to the total educational process in which a student is involved. The educator as teacher sees the classroom processes as one aspect of the whole program of a school. The administrator as educator makes his decisions in terms of their relation to the whole educational process—to how they will influence each pupil in his situation, and not only how they will agree with one or another political group in the community. The educator understands the dynamic elements in the lives of both students and teachers and does not try to cut through them with irrelevancies or short-circuit them in hopes of speeding education faster than it is able to go. He understands the influence of external setting upon the responses of students and takes responsibility to adapt the structures of the institution or program in order to make them more conducive to the type of learning that is intended.

DISCUSSION

The methods to express each basic teaching process are available in vast profusion. Their use depends upon the teacher's skill with one or another, and upon his judgment of appropriateness on a particular occasion. This factor of selective judgment may be illustrated in analyzing the uses of "the discussion method."

Discussion is an important instrument of social relations and group decision, but it is a very difficult teaching method. Its complexity becomes clear when we examine the many different kinds of discussion, the different roles demanded of the teacher or leader, and the implications of each for understanding of man and his relation to community.

Fixed-end. Discussion is often employed in relation with indoctrination when, following a lecture, questions may be asked to clarify meanings, to reveal misunderstandings, or to explore implications. Discussion is also employed to help people understand policies or programs already determined, giving those who are to carry them out an opportunity to question the reasons for the policy and to review the problems involved in implementation. When the end is fixed the function of the leader or teacher becomes one of answering questions, sometimes persuading, but always employing the discussion to obtain acceptance. The function is essentially defensive and may easily become manipulative.

Open-ended. There are several types of open-ended discussion commonly used. One is *topical,* which might be employed in an interview when opinions are sought about a product, a job, a subject, or when trying to find out present knowledge of a person, or when both sides are to be presented. The teacher or leader exercises direction only to keep the discussion on the topic and to bring out ideas for everyone involved. Another type is *brainstorming,*[58] which focuses attention on eliciting as many different ideas or suggestions as possible about a common theme. Techniques have been formalized for brainstorming which limit the leader to a police function of maintaining a fast pace of participation, and not allowing anyone to speak in defense of his ideas, but in other less formalized situations the leader would have more flexibility. A third type of open-ended discussion is *conversation* in which the leader (or host) is concerned with the relationship of the participants as well as with the dynamics of their thinking. The fourth is the totally unstructured *bull session* where no leader is necessary, where any topic may be discussed, and where the natural dynamics of group relationships have free play.

The use of open-ended discussion as an educational method is difficult because it cannot be anticipated and prepared for. The teacher takes occasions that arise to probe for meaning or assist in clarification of issues, but because the teacher must be essentially a member of the group he cannot control the direction or pace of the discussion.

Problem-solving. Discussion is employed in many fields in the solving of problems—political, scientific, religious, social, etc. In some instances, the discussion is *advisory,* as when a staff discusses all aspects of a problem, but the executive has to make a decision; then only the executive is responsible, the staff is not. In other instances, the discussion precedes a group decision, as when a board of trustees meets and every member is responsible for the consequences of the decision. In either case, the teacher or leader may or may not have more competency than others involved, but the difference of function is clear. In group decisions there are several ways by which the decision is actually reached—by majority vote, by consensus, or "sense of the meeting."

Legislative. In Congress, at the annual meeting of a union, at the general assembly of a church, or in the United Nations, discussion pointed toward enacting legislation may be quite different from other forms. Usually, it is limited by specific rules of procedure (whether Robert's Rules or other), which attempt to be objective, yet at the same time it is conducted in the setting of political pressures and designed to obtain groupings of support for passing or defeating a proposal. This legislative discussion is pointed toward *majority rule.* In other settings the discussion is pointed toward *consensus* when, at least ostensibly, there are no political power blocs, where the pressure for decision is not so great, and where votes may never be taken because agreement is arrived at by adjustments among all participants.[59]

Though consensus may appear to respect all persons, it may be as subject to manipulation as is majority rule, when one person dominates by tradition, persuasion, or special competency. Legislative discussion is part of the democratic process, which respects the rights and point of view of the minority, but it depends upon acceptance by the society at large if its processes are to be effective. When a large proportion of the population in a country no longer trusts the process, discussion becomes irrelevant.

The person responsible for directing these two types of discussion has very different responsibilities. Under majority rule, a chairman or leader has a primary responsibility to protect the right of every point of view to be heard, whereas in seeking consensus his responsibility is to see that the position adopted is fair to all points of view.

Legislative discussion is employed in all types of educational institutions but is seldom used as a teaching method except in instances where a teacher provides for collective decisions by students of what they are going to do: a drama class might vote on the play it wishes to produce or a geology class may select by vote the site of a field trip.

Socratic Dialogue. Perhaps the most difficult of all forms of discussion is the use of Socratic dialogue as a way of teaching. Socratic dialogue is not the employment of the "leading question" which may, through skillful manipulation, prompt a person by consistent and logical steps into a position he does not really hold. It does imply that the student has within him the answer to the question though he does not recognize it, so the teacher (or Socrates)[60] offers the answer and the student recognizes that it expresses what he already thought. For the teacher, this form implies such profound understanding of the subject that he can begin wherever the student is in his knowledge and guide by simple, logical steps to a full comprehension which the student can grasp at each step. This implies, of course, that each subject can be thus "programmed" in logical order, and that learning is essentially "remembering."

Debate. Debate is a form of discussion, sometimes used in the legislative process, which is designed to sharpen all the aspects of an issue or a problem. In formal debates, objective rules of procedure guide the discussion, and the direction by a leader is minimal. In a classroom, debate may be used when there are no special rules, but the objective of the leader is to see that the issues are sharply defined so that each person can decide where he stands. Such debate may not need to have any immediate resolution.

Question and Answer. How often lecture announcements read: "After the lecture there will be time for discussion." But after the lecture what happens is a question and answer session. This form can, however, be a constructive form of discussion. On the one hand, students may ask the questions—to clarify the points made, to challenge the speaker, to suggest insights that were missed, etc., all of which may be valuable both to teacher and to student. On the other hand, the teacher may ask the questions—to see if the major points were understood, to see how students respond or appropriate what was said. Question and answer discussion requires as careful advance preparation as any other teaching method.

Integrative. Some discussion is employed in relation to a variety of experiences rather than to one, when the object is the relating of new ideas and experiences to those the student already holds. As in other types an effort is made to focus issues involved, but great care and sensitivity are needed on the part of leader or teacher to keep from suggesting invalid integration, to accept the pace of the student, and to respect his own ideas of what fits together in his life.

There is no automatic relation between particular discussion methods and the various basic teaching processes. Discussion would more likely be used by teachers who want to establish a reactive, interactive, or demonstrative relationship with students in a class. Fixed-end use of questions and answers, or the Socratic method, may be employed by teachers establishing a distributive or directive process. In other words, the way the method is employed is more determinative of the basic process than is the type of method selected.

"Discussion" can mean any one of the types suggested. Each has validity in appropriate circumstances, and each makes specific demands upon a teacher or leader. Within the varied activities of a creative class, the teacher may employ debate between two groups reporting on research, legislative discussion (majority rule) to decide the procedure in a class project, Socratic dialogue with a student unable to keep up with other students, fixed-end discussion to help students understand proper laboratory techniques, and question and answer to discern what the students have understood of the semester's work.

Discussion, therefore, is not necessarily a more appropriate method than others in effective education. Its use, as with other methods, depends upon the teacher's interpretation of the situation and the end toward which the educational occasion is directed, and upon the teacher's competency in understanding and using the various possibilities of each method. Thus the method employed in any occasion should serve the responsible intention of the teacher.

Other techniques and methods of education require a comparable analytic clarification to see their place in the total field of education.

Chapter VI

PRESCRIPTS

EACH PERSON will learn many things during his lifetime, yet most societies, nations, or groups, select some things as particularly important for their members to learn. They may be certain ideas that each citizen is expected to adopt or certain ways of doing things that are to become normative within a nation or group. Education is a system by which a society expresses its expectations for such particular learning.

Each society also develops a rationale to justify its expectations. The claims of patriotism may lead to a particular interpretation of historical events. The needs of economic development may require more teaching of particular technical skills. Such claims of a society press its educational system to function as a producer of certain conduct, ideas, or beliefs.

Educational prescripts express the political realities of a society when the educational system becomes an instrument by which those in power attempt to form the ideas, behavior, or beliefs of all others. On the other hand, educational prescripts may be interpreted as a rational or logical process by which a society attempts to serve its own most obvious needs of adaptation, expansion, or survival. Education is a prescriptive activity from the perspective of those who initiate or conduct educational programs.

Educational prescripts imply selection, from among the limitless number of things a person may learn, of particular matters to be learned and of a rationalization about why it is important to learn these things. In this sense every educational goal or purpose is the expression of a value system within a society, nation, or group.[61]

Complexity of objective is a distinguishing mark of education. As indicated in the previous chapter, education always involves three stages of processes. Each of these is informed (implicitly or explicitly) by objectives, yet at the same time all are pointed toward a further stage of purpose, namely, what the learners are to do *after* the educational experience.

Thus education must be recognized as a four-stage social activity in terms of its objectives. These may be seen as consecutive "in-order-thats": certain things are done in systemizing in-order-that teachers may do certain things, in-order-that students may do certain things, and in-order-that, beyond the educational occasion, students may act, think, or believe in certain ways.

Education is a prescriptive activity in that while its requirements are directed toward both teachers and learners, it usually implies an intention beyond the educational activities themselves. A legislative body might be considered to engage in prescriptive activity when laws are passed to direct the conduct of citizens. However, in education such first-stage prescripts are only functional or enabling, for their objective is pointed beyond the conduct of teachers or learners within the educational activity. Medicine provides a more adequate analogy, for instance, in a doctor's activity of giving a prescription to a patient. Taking pills or doing exercises or gargling an antiseptic are first-step objectives. They point toward a physical condition beyond themselves. The doctor cannot prescribe health, but his prescription hopefully enables a patient to get well. Education is prescriptive in somewhat the same sense.

Of course it is possible for a doctor to attempt to control, through the prescriptive activity, what the physical condition of the patient will be after he takes his medicine. Similarly in education, many activities are conducted not only with the intention of prescribing what a learner does within the educational occasion but also with the intention of controlling what he will do, think, or believe afterward. Such activities would then be appropriately called normative as well as prescriptive.

The possibilities of such control need to be examined in relation to the interpretation of appropriation and understanding in a subsequent chapter, but it is obvious that many education programs have such fourth-stage normative prescripts. However, it is important to note that these are not the only goals in education, for each stage of educational processes is subject to prescriptive requirements.

In a state board of education the *systemizing stage* of processes incorporates many prescripts for the operation of local boards of education, for types and sizes of school buildings, for procedures in handling money, for record-keeping, for courses of study. These prescripts are like the "regulations" of any large company or bureaucracy, yet they are important and cannot be subsumed under a general statement of fourth-stage aims. The bureaucratic prescripts may be viewed as primary enablers of the activities eventually to take place in a classroom, but they also develop their own validating standards because each educational institution (as was noted previously) incorporates a variety of objectives.

Whether in simple social settings or in the complex structures of a contemporary national ministry of education, the systemizing stage is deeply involved in developing prescripts for what is to be done in the pedagogic stage. In tribal activities it may be the chief of the tribe or the tribal council that prescribes what one of their number, or a medicine man, or a specially selected and trained individual is to do in preparing boys for the initiation rites. The patterns, as pointed out in the previous chapter, may have been handed down from generation to generation, but they are reconfirmed as prescripts with binding obligation. The prescripts are guides to pedagogic processes and also become the basis for the standards by which those processes are to be evaluated. In some things the tribal council will judge the "teacher" by the conduct of the learners, but in other things the evidence of what is learned may not become obvious for many years, yet the "teacher" will be judged by how well he observed the pedagogic prescripts.

The *pedagogic stage* of processes, also, is marked by distinctive prescripts. These identify the able counselor, the skilled lecturer, the competent authority in his field, the good classroom teacher. Here, too, the prescripts are guides to appropriate action as well as standards for judging ability. These prescripts may have no relation to the competency or conduct of students after they leave the classroom; they stand by themselves derived from a priori objectives on the part of the systemizers and of the teacher's own image of what is appropriate to the classroom.

The *curricular stage* of processes always incorporates many prescripts for learners. These prescripts may include conduct in the "class," reading assignments, recitations, exercises, demonstrations, projects, examinations. They may incorporate particular teacher-student relationships, or certain pupil attitudes, or cleanliness, or special attire, or demonstrations of respect. Within this stage they provide standards for judging the good student. Some of the requirements within a school may be modeled after requirements that society will make later, but others may be intra-educational prescripts considered essential to the smooth functioning of an educational system, or for the general welfare and safety of students.

Finally, in the fourth stage are those expectations or requirements which are specifically pointed toward their practice after the educational occasion, what may be called the *alumnal stage*. These include such matters as technical skills that a barber must display in his occupation, or the techniques a sculptor uses in his profession, or the knowledge a lawyer must display in order to win a case in court, or the girl's skill in baking cakes, or the Indian's skill in making canoes. The fourth-stage prescripts may also include political ideologies, moral standards, or theological beliefs which the learner is expected to hold through his later life.[62] Most societies imply a second phase beyond the personal one in the alumnal stage, that is, that the conduct, beliefs or ways of thinking of the alumni should be proper in-order-that the aesthetic aspects of society may be improved, or that the nation may survive, or that industry may be more efficient. In other words, even in the fourth stage there may be a distinction between functional and ultimate ends.

From this brief analysis of the relation of objectives or pre-scripts to the various stages of educational processes, the complexity of educational "purposes" becomes more obvious. The most frequent and oversimplified assumption is that "the aims of education" refer only to the alumnal stage. Yet obviously the alumnal-stage prescripts cannot be accomplished unless each prior stage makes an effective contribution to that long-range objective. Actually, one of the most difficult problems in all educational systems is to correlate the prescripts of the various stages to each other. Vitality in educational development often is the product of tension between the prescripts of the several stages, as well as of conflicts between different philosophical points of view.

The various objectives of education are *conditional* in relation to each other. That is, the influence of circumstances in each stage moves in both directions. It is commonly accepted that the prescripts of the systemizing stage will influence the pedagogic, curricular, and alumnal stages. Similarly, though less commonly understood, the conditions under which an alumnus must conduct a trade, practice his profession, or employ his talent may by a reverse flow or feedback make claims upon objectives of the prior stages. One of the marks of psychological sensitivity and educational efficiency is the awareness on the part of educators of the situation in which an alumnus will find himself and the problems he is likely to have in using what he has appropriated from his educational experience.

ALUMNAL OBJECTIVES

Consideration of educational aims usually focuses only upon goals for the alumnal stage, on the assumption that educational systems are a type of factory geared to produce a particular product.[63] Three types of product, or "ends," each with varied emphases, find expression in many different societies: (1) things to do—particular activities; (2) things to believe—commitments; and (3) things to know—cognition. The implications of such a "production model" for education will be examined later when exploring the relation of goals to processes, but here the types of long-range objectives need to be clarified.

Activity. The simplest, and perhaps the most basic, activity sought in education is the development of *skills.*[64] Simple teaching of language begins very early and is amplified in later education. The same is true of bodily care and development. The mother who shows her daughter how to cook a meal and the father who shows his son how to handle a knife are teaching their children skills they think are important for them to learn. Every society has patterns for the activities that maintain life, so whether or not other ends may be sought in its educational activities, the teaching of elementary skills would be essential. From the simplest to the most advanced societies there are increasingly extensive and complex levels of technical skills required to provide food, shelter, transportation, and all the other essentials for maintaining life.

For the individual learning the skill, this is also an essential economic activity by which to support himself and his family. Some members of a nation are trained to administer the affairs of the government, and others to provide military and police protection, but each activity also gives income to the breadwinner and his family.

In advanced societies the range of skills may expand into all types of technical, political, and academic areas that either maintain the society or give outlet for individual creativity and interest. A developing country may work out a carefully rationalized plan for the production of specific skills for selected industries and expect the school system to produce them.[65] Or a society may focus on "thinking" as a skill that schools should develop. Extensive efforts have been made to analyze and classify the different types of thinking and explore their relation to the total scope of education.[66] Thus the intention of an educational program to develop technical skills may include aspects from many ranges of learning in addition to the technical, such as bodily development, aesthetic preference, and social relationships.

Social viability also requires common *behavior,* and each society employs a wide variety of mechanisms to maintain its general behavioral patterns. One of these mechanisms is its educational system. Within such a system the behavior of students is directed in order to allow the system to operate effectively, but also as a pattern to be followed beyond the educational activity. Such long-range prescripts usually assume that the educational program will present the rationale and principles that should govern behavior, whether explained in terms of moral rules or in terms of social utility. In some societies, however, the concern of educational activities is to instill habits of behavior, whether the principles are understood or not, in childhood so that they will be practiced by the members in later years. The behavior sought may range from personal grooming to service in the Peace Corps overseas.

Educational programs are sometimes expected to be agencies for group or mass activity. The use of schools to initiate *social change* has been the intention of leaders in many societies. Since educational institutions tend to be inherently conservative there is often a conflict between the social posture that the school represents and the new social order to which the schools are asked to contribute.[67] Yet the more centralized the organization of the schools, the more possibility that they may be used for either the promotion or the prevention of social change.

The long-range educational goal of some societies has been a *continuing process* of education, so that in a sense there would be no alumnal stage.[68] A particularly heated debate of twentieth-century education has centered on the issue of whether the ends of education transcend the process itself, and if so, the nature of that transcendent frame of reference. Obviously the commitment to a right "process," whatever the product may be, assumes a particular view of the nature of man and of the world. Progressive education was based on a naturalist view of man so that growth was the continuing process that education was to encourage, and growth would continue throughout life.[69] More recently greater emphasis has been placed upon the goal of developing "the ability to think." If the goal of education is developing "the ability to think," there is no guidance within this objective for what is most valuable to think about. Many who reacted against this emphasis on "process" tended to assume that process could be independent of subject matter, in an oversimplified separation of "method" from "content." Thus the alumnal goals that attempt to prescribe things to do—activities—cannot be understood except in relation to other values or goals of society.

Commitment. If the concern for the basic necessities of food, clothing, and shelter has been satisfied sufficiently to maintain life, every society is concerned also with the learning of its constitutive beliefs. The story of its origin and the mythical account of its character are passed on from generation to generation as an essential element for the preservation of the society. Sometimes the beliefs are more important than food, shelter, or clothing, and a society or group may fight an obviously losing war to protect its ideology.[70]

Each society develops educational procedures of some kind, schools or tribal initiation rites, or legends and songs, in an attempt to assure the right beliefs on the part of its members. In more complex and pluralistic societies there may be many groups (political parties, churches, lodges, philosophical societies, professional groups, fraternities) devoted to transmitting and reinterpreting these right beliefs around which group loyalties are maintained. Some groups describe their beliefs as "the truth" and teach their adherents that only what they believe is true. Such groups tend to be aggressive in attempting to win adherents so that they expect their educational activities to be a form of spiritual conquest.

Each child "belongs" to the family, tribe, or society into which he is born and before he is verbal has become indelibly configured by the culture of which he is a part. But often a nation or a society, or a group within a community, is not satisfied with the fact of this belonging; it wants the person to understand what he belongs to and why, to participate in the myths of the tribe or nation and to celebrate the events that are held up as explanations of its distinctiveness. So these nations, societies, or groups may employ their educational system as one means of inducting a person into the characteristic commitments of the society or nation.

A person may belong to other types of groups, associations, or clubs, by choice, but the inductive activities can be equally important and educational programs may be required as a means of such induction.

Most societies either consciously or unconsciously hold up a model for their young and exalt a personality type as an expression of what they think a person should be. Part of the intention of their educational activities is to produce alumni committed to becoming such persons. Whether an English "gentleman," or a Black Power "militant," or a skilled "spy," or a "clergyman" who will be an example to others—in each case their education implies commitment to being a certain type of person. In a broader sense, since each society requires common effort to survive, a major emphasis in most education is upon the necessity and virtue of cooperation and conformity. On the other hand, the aim of personality development may be of a much more general nature. Rather than the fabrication of a particular model, some societies have attempted to design educational programs with the goal of developing the creative possibilities of each individual. Historically the commitment to the humanities or the liberal arts has been a means for developing a fully human being.

Cognition. Each type of long-range educational goal requires certain kinds of "knowledge" in relation to skills, beliefs, behavior, or personality. In some societies the content of the educational program is essentially utilitarian knowledge, while others have developed a commitment to the value of knowledge in itself. Such a view is expressed in the idea that the function of education is the search for truth. In some highly technical societies the distinction between pure and applied research may imply a somewhat higher value for applied research, while pure research is thought of as devoted to knowledge (truth) for its own sake.

The goal of knowledge may be related to the goal of activity in the optimistic conviction that if a person knows what is right he will be able to do it, or if he knows the rules he will be able to apply them in particular situations. This was one argument in defense of memorizing as the principal method of education for so many centuries. But knowledge must be examined in relation to understanding, as will be done in the next chapter.

The three types of alumnal prescripts for education may be discerned singly or in combination in many different kinds of education programs—within whole nations or societies, in tribes, in industries, in government agencies, and in individual schools. One or more of these types is implied in every educational activity whether made explicit or not. They can be discerned in the expectations of those who sponsor the program or system, in the images that teachers or students bring with them, as well as in the activities conducted or the material studied.

All education is a prescriptive activity, but this indicates only one aspect of the equation of this social phenomenon. To articulate a goal is but one step in the longer and more complex process of designing an educational system or developing an educational institution, and both the processes and the institutional structures control the implementation and require the continuing reformulation of the prescripts.[71] But the efficacy of prescription depends upon appropriation by students, for from their perspective education is an appropriative activity.

When prescripts specify what a person is to learn, a basic moral question is raised about the right of an individual or a system to require particular learning. Every teacher is making a moral as well as an academic decision when he seeks to change the ideas or behavior of another person. Since each learner comes to an educational occasion with a set of interpretations of his life's experience, what right does a teacher have to change that interpretation?

Educational systems may rationalize their answers to this question in different ways, and each answer reflects a basic philosophical position. The answer may be based on the assumption that the majority has an inherent right to specify what all students will learn, or that the educational authorities have special knowledge of the truth to be transmitted, or that the validity of what is being taught is self-evident. Whatever the rationalization, the issue remains, for each requirement for learning is a moral decision.

Even in systems where the objective is to confront students with ideas or experiences and not to try to control their appropriation, teachers are caught in the same moral responsibility. The alternatives of readings recommended, the variety of experiences planned, the frequency or strength of confrontations incorporated into a study program, all tend to control the possibilities of response by students. Each forces the teacher to make a moral decision that may profoundly affect the lives of the students.

Both of these aspects of the moral dimensions of education may be illustrated in an attempt by middle-class schools to study the problem of poverty. Why do they plan the course? Do they assume that middle-class children do not know about poverty but ought to, therefore they need knowledge; or that middle-class children are prejudiced toward the poor, therefore they need a change of attitude; or that middle-class children are insulated from reality, therefore they need to be exposed to direct contact with slum situations? The reason for such a course and the objective toward which it is directed grow from these basic assumptions and each one implies a moral judgment upon the knowledge, attitudes, or experience of the children involved.

In developing such a course, the planners would have to select the books to read, choose what activities to include, decide whether poor children should be invited to attend the class or the class should go to visit a poor section of a city, and also decide what the class would discuss or write about. Each of these decisions could have far-reaching effects upon the life of each student. Then when a teacher conducts the course he interprets the text material, he makes comments in discussion, he expresses some kind of attitude toward student comments or toward the situation of the poor—and in each of these he, too, can affect the lives of the students in one way or another. So each act of a teacher raises moral questions of his right to such influence.

Every educational decision is at the same time a moral decision. Every educational prescript implies moral judgments. Thus the basic dimension of education is not so much in its conscious promotion of moral precepts as it is in the inherent moral posture which any educational agency abrogates to itself in its decisions to change the ideas, convictions, or behavior of learners.

In consequence of this inherent dimension of what they do, competent educators are aware of the moral implications of their academic decisions just as competent legislators, industrialists, or judges are aware of the moral dimensions of every professional decision.[72]

Chapter VII

UNDERSTANDING

CHAPTER I identified ten ranges of learning that most people are expected to acquire during their lifetime. Some of these ranges need no special institution for teaching. Others are clearly matters of acceptable or unacceptable activity, and an educational institution may contribute to the society by helping a person to comprehend the reason for standards or laws or social patterns. However, education always implies that beyond the particular conduct or skill there is a deeper meaning and that it is the peculiar responsibility of education to engage a person in trying to understand that meaning of his own existence.

What does it mean to "understand"? Each philosophical position has its own answer to that question. But is it possible to describe "understanding" in phenomenological terms without taking one or another of these positions? This question is as important in developing a program of education as it is in developing a philosophy of education.

Obviously the twentieth century is a pluralistic age. No society can escape contact with the world around, and so within every society are many competing views and commitments. If a society or a school system could assume that all participants hold a common educational philosophy, then it might be justified in trying to develop educational programs around a single view of "understanding." But this is not a possibility anywhere in the world, even under the most tightly controlled totalitarian systems. It is not possible to set up an educational system of any size in which all sponsors, administrators, and teachers hold the same educational commitments.

Every philosophy of education, and every educational system whether large or small, is pressed by varieties of points of view on all educational matters, and this includes varieties of views on what it means to understand. Education can never operate in isolation from surrounding cultures. Other societal relationships of administrators, teachers, and students are reflected in what is thought and done within the educational program. In order to see the place that epistemological positions take in the total process of education a descriptive approach is more helpful than the prescriptive.

If, then, on the assumption that all education is conducted in a pluralistic setting, and some *modus operandi* and rationale is needed in order to fulfill its diverse responsibilities, the starting point for that development is a careful delineation of the situation and possibilities being faced.

Understanding is an activity that reflects a particular relationship to that which is known. In each range of learning there are internal and external dimensions; that is, to know implies some relation to that which is outside oneself, and also implies a knowledge of the relating self. Without attempting to specify the limits of what may be known, it is clear that knowing is a kind of *activity* of a knower, not an impersonal absorption of facts.

Understanding is a self-conscious recognition of knowledge. Knowledge may be acquired and employed without consciousness of that activity. Understanding is a more complex act by which the knowledge is placed in some kind of frame of reference. To understand that heat rises is to comprehend the action of heat in relation to its surrounding. To understand the love of mother and child is to see the parent-child relationship discriminated from other kinds of relationships. To understand why two plus two is four is to comprehend the relation of those numbers to each other and the place of addition in the larger activity of numbers. To know may be a direct action; to understand is a reflective action that does something about that which is known.

Understanding goes beyond knowledge and implies a relationship of personal response to what is known. So what is known is personalized in the process of understanding, and the understanding that a person has cannot be transmitted as such to another person without being repersonalized. A teacher's understanding of why Washington has been called "the father of our country" is a personal understanding that can only be approximated in his attempts to communicate that understanding to students, and what the students appropriate will be their own personal coloring of the meaning of that phrase.

In other words, understanding, like knowledge, is an activity of a knower that cannot be transmitted from teacher to student without being acted upon by the student. When what a student does about the teacher's ideas becomes a conscious activity, when he comprehends why the teacher thinks as he does, then he understands his teacher. When he comprehends why apples fall from trees then he understands gravity. When he comprehends why he reacts as he does to his teacher or to particular subjects then he understands himself.

Self-conscious understanding requires articulation at least to the extent of a person's being able to think about what is going on. In most educational programs this articulation includes the ability to express one's interpretation of meaning to another person in communicable form. But understanding and meaning are not the same thing. A picture may mean a great deal to a boy who does not understand it. He does not understand why it means so much to him, so he cannot communicate either the meaning or the reason for his lack of understanding of it.

Understanding is a processual dimension of knowledge. It is an activity of comprehension, the comprehension of relationship or cause or meaning, not a static product of thinking.

While understanding is a reflective activity of a learner, it is not usually an activity that a learner can conduct within himself. There is always an implicit encounter with otherness. To understand a poem inevitably involves an encounter with the poem. To understand a mathematical process requires some encounter with what others have done before or with some event in which that mathematical process was involved.[73] To understand the forces of nature requires an encounter with nature.

The encounter is between the matter to be understood and the total person of a learner. Understanding is an activity of the whole person. Every aspect of one's background, intelligence, experience, aesthetic sense, etc., is involved in understanding anything. It is a *person* who understands;[74] he understands from within the context of who and where he is; he understands in his own way and from his own location in space and time. He cannot understand a picture, a historical event, a mathematical operation as someone else understands them. His understanding is an activity of his whole person, with its quirks and foibles, its prejudices and blindness, its values and passions. Others can ask him to repeat what they have said to him, even to translate it into his own terminology, but repeating does not prove understanding. He has to see what it is in terms of its relation to his own life before he can understand it.

For instance, in bodily development, he can understand in two ways: he can understand the principles of what makes for good health and bodily safety, that is, he can understand *about* bodily development; and he can understand through trying to apply the principles to himself. He understands the danger of smoking in a different way when he gets cancer of the throat than when he reads statistics about other people who get throat cancer from smoking.

So in all other ranges of learning. Understanding "about" the matter is not necessarily impersonal; rather it can mean understanding in terms of the way the matter applies to all people in contrast to existential understanding. Even general understanding is personal in the sense that the whole person is involved in the act of such understanding. Existential understanding is personal not only in the fact that it is subjective, but more importantly in the sense of the involvement of the whole person.

Understanding is an activity that may be described in five steps:

Openness. An openness to consider the matter. If there is resistance even to consideration, then understanding is, for the moment, automatically precluded.

Recognition. In this second step one might say, "I see what you are talking about." Recognition is an identification of the matter and placing it in some range of context for consideration.

Clarification. With further examination the matter is distinguished for what it is in itself and one can say, "What you are saying is clear to me."

Comprehension. After the matter has become clear comes the grasping, the comprehending, of what is involved in the event or process, and one may then say, "I know it."

Appropriation. But there is another level or step in which a person realizes the relation of the matter to himself, the way it involves him as a person and may influence his life. Then he may say, "I understand what you say," meaning that he allows it to become a part of his life.

A variety of psychological and sociological factors may be involved for each student in each of these five steps. Openness or closedness will be the product of his exterior or interior setting. Motivations, interests, prejudices, fears, curiosity, intuition, parental repression, peer group pressure, provincial experience, level of intelligence, creativity—all may be interacting within a person in each step. Efforts to help a person understand, therefore, must begin with a realistic appraisal of the influence of the internal and external settings in this particular occasion as well as with some awareness of the steps by which a person develops understanding.[75] The presence of a student in a classroom is no assurance of his openness any more than a "yes" answer to the question, "Do you understand what I am saying?" is a guarantee that he does.

While these many factors of the internal and external setting of a student are important to take into account, controlling or manipulating these factors is not the teacher's distinctive contribution to a student's understanding. Rather, the teacher needs to recognize that these factors describe the setting within which the student understands; they shape the way of his understanding; they pattern the influence of his understanding upon his life. These, then, are conditions within which a teacher performs his distinctive function. Within them the student gains understanding as a creative activity on his own part.[76]

PERSPECTIVE

Education's distinctive contribution toward understanding is in providing perspective. Learning goes on all the time, and though all learning involves learning "something," [77] this can be done without a conscious effort to direct that learning. An educational process always involves someone else besides the learner who has intentions for the learner. This "other" person inevitably represents another perspective upon whatever is being studied.[78]

To put things in perspective implies that each matter being considered relates to other matters, and the way things are interrelated is a crucial factor in understanding each of them.[79] Problems of radiation in space are related to drinking water on earth and to bone structure of human beings. There is an integrality of all things which requires discrimination for understanding, and the process of discrimination is one of identifying how things are related to each other within some frame of reference.

Perspective may move either macrocosmically or microcosmically, either by appreciating larger and larger frames of reference, or, if beginning in the larger frame, by moving progressively to smaller and smaller ranges.[80] Understanding one day in a historical event depends upon one's perspective in the context of a broader sweep of that which preceded or follows that day. Understanding a painting requires a broader perspective provided by knowing the movements that it represents, the artist, the techniques employed, as well as the form and color within the specific art object.

Macrocosmic frames of reference are usually a contribution of imagination or the contribution of other persons with broader knowledge and experience. For instance, the development of synthetic rubber in the United States has had a profound effect upon the economy of Malaysia, but what is that effect? A student can either try to imagine the effects or he can seek for someone who has documented the effects or participated in them. While it is salutary to imagine the relation of one event with another, there is grave danger in such imagination,[81] for there is no way that a person in the United States can comprehend the fabric of life in Malaysia and the impact of the loss of income upon that life. Thus there must be a ceaseless pressure to move from imagination to reality. One of the functions of the teacher, hopefully better informed than the students, is continually to question the products of imagination and press for understanding based upon involvement with reality.

Perspective functions comparatively or by analogy.[82] Understanding may derive from comparing this painting with another painting, this historical event to another one. Are they similar or different, and in what way? Analogical thinking is important in every subject, and is a useful tool for the teacher in every field, for comparing is a natural process of thinking. Perspective may be more than comparing or contrasting likes and unlikes; it implies a shift of frame of reference, different realms of meaning, other angles of vision, alternate sets of relationships. It may be a product of divergent as well as of convergent thinking.

Yet whether the perspective is spatial (to larger frames of reference) or comparative, every person has a threshold beyond which he is unable to perceive either relationship or comparison. This apperceptive limitation may be one of cultural deprivation, or intellectual level, or prior experience. Whichever it is, it is important for the teacher to discern the apperceptive limitations of his students at each step in their educational development. Apperception is not a static quality; it can be enlarged, and the teacher may take steps to assist such enlargement before going on with other steps of an educational program.

The most commonly employed perspective in education is developmental or historical. In most fields the student is helped to understand by bringing a historical perspective to bear upon art forms, the making of automobiles, the development of mathematics, or the varieties of philosophies. To discern what comes before and after, or to trace past events and anticipate future repercussions is to gain perspective.

Perspective may move out in successive levels so that education might be described as a process of bringing larger and larger forms of reference to bear upon a particular matter. When the intention of education is to provide the understanding necessary for responsible decision-making, then the perspective employed may be enlarged to include every relevant factor. Such a movement eventually raises the question of metaphysical and transcendent frames of reference.

Every person lives by an implicit philosophy of life. If theology is the activity of thinking about or speaking about one's view of that which is ultimate (in religious terms—god), then implicitly every person has a theology. The highest and most inclusive perspective that can be brought to bear, thus, would be a metaphysical or theological perspective. All education is conducted within some assumptions about man, the world, time, the ultimate meaning of existence. Usually these are not articulated or considered. When education fails to consider them it is not bringing all relevant factors into the perspective of its teaching.

Perspective in education is a product both of the educational context and of the activity carried on within a particular educational occasion. The presence of a teacher, of others in a class, of classroom processes, of resource materials—these all involve other perspectives to which a student is exposed. Each teacher introduces ideas and activities that articulate yet other perspectives. Thus exposed, the student responds in some way. If he is closed, he will reject and defend what he already thinks. If he is open, he will consider and examine other points of view and decide whether any are acceptable, and if so, which ones or which combination of views he will appropriate.

Thus the principal means by which educational activities provide perspective are by personal encounter, appropriate projection of imagination, introduction of new material for thinking, articulating of ultimate frames of reference, and sharing in new activities of experience.[83]

The content of perspective, particularly in upper levels of education, is to be found in the interaction of disciplines. In part an academic discipline is a particular perspective on reality.[84] To look at existence through the methodologies of the physicist is not to encounter a different world from history, but it is to look at the same world from a distinctive perspective. For the physicist, therefore, the study of history brings a different perspective, as it does for the artist or the philosopher. The function of interdisciplinary study for many people is an effort to recapture the lost world of a medieval hegemony of knowledge maintained by the power of an international institution. Such unity is not possible now and probably will never be possible again as it was in the fourteenth century. Even then the "unity of knowledge" was provincial; it left out Moorish Spain, all of Africa, Asia, and the Americas. In the twentieth century everyone in the world is exposed to everything happening on earth. There is no way to protect anyone from ideas, convictions, practices, hopes, and dreams of others. And the common humanity is far too creative to allow one mode of thought to capture the minds of all men.

So the contribution of interdisciplinary study and encounter in the twentieth century is to clarify not to integrate. Contrast is needed as well as comparison, difference as well as similarity. In providing perspective, education can offer depth and penetration of a subject. And in the light of a new perspective old ideas may gain new power or may have to be discarded. To be a student is to be engaged in a continuing process of accepting, revising, or rejecting ideas in the light of the perspective that one's education brings to bear upon them.

Chapter VIII

PHILOSOPHY

EVERY PERSON has a philosophy of education whether he realizes it or not, and whether he has had occasion to formulate it systematically or not. Each person has some idea of what education is, how people learn, what teachers do, how schools are organized, and what would be appropriate goals. These educational ideas may be based upon his experiences and ideas he has gained from others, but they also reflect his interpretation of reality and his own view of the meaning of existence.

Every educational activity expresses a philosophy of education whether the participants realize it or not, and whether its planners based that activity upon an explicit formulation of their views or not. Education is a social activity requiring cooperation by groups of people, so there needs to be at least minimal agreement upon organizational patterns, content, and general objectives. Since each of these matters may be interpreted in various ways, most educational systems incorporate a wide variety of philosophies of education. For this reason the attempt to spell out a particular philosophy and then implement it consistently in an educational program shows a crude disregard for the complex ways in which philosophy and education are intertwined.

The term "philosophy" often implies a fixed stance rooted in verities that cannot be changed, but the work of philosophy is not static. It is an intellectual activity intended to identify and clarify basic ideas and convictions about a particular matter. It is a reflective activity, reexamining present views in the light of the thinking of others or of new experiences. Philosophical activity is an attempt to be logical and systematic, self-consciously exploring how ideas fit together into a whole. The result of such activity may be called "a philosophy," but every formulation is immediately confronted by new ideas and new experiences, so the reflection will be repeated. Thus the attempt to arrive at a fixed set of beliefs to hold against future change is always frustrated by continuing philosophical activity.

Clarifying one's philosophy of education is more a matter of discovery than of construction. When an attempt is made to describe a philosophy of education one usually puts together ideas drawn from recognized authorities, concepts that seem to fit together in logical order, or principles implied from one's general philosophical commitments. In this way one constructs a philosophy of education. The danger in such a process, however, is that in striving to take many factors into account, in trying to maintain logical consistency, or in attempting to follow respected authorities, one covers up the convictions by which he actually lives. A more valid first step is the self-disciplined exploring of the implicit philosophy one already holds. And since a philosophy of education is an application of one's basic philosophical position to a particular area of social activity, it cannot be separated from one's more basic commitments.[85]

FUNCTIONS

An educational activity is a system of interacting steps. Though there is an accepted sequence by which an educational activity is structured, planned, conducted, and evaluated, the interaction between the steps is dialectical rather than linear. In other words, the structure both influences and is part of the content; goals are qualified by the methods available to attain them; and the learning capacity of students affects the conduct of teachers.

The interaction between the steps can be seen in the complex operations of a program, but may be viewed on a deeper level in the philosophical roots for each step. Philosophy is an inherent component of any educational system and performs certain distinctive functions within the system.

One essential function of a philosophy of education is to provide the interpretation of man's social interrelationships as the frame of reference for determining the structures within which this particular kind of social activity may be carried on. Because education tends to be highly traditional, its activities are usually planned within existing structures without questioning their validity. When there is occasion, however, to adopt or design new structures, the decisions reflect basic assumptions about the appropriate structures of human existence. A social activity such as education requires cooperation of many individuals. Each person involved in setting up structures for educational planning and activity has convictions about the proper arrangements that make it possible for persons with different but interdependent responsibilities to work together. A person must operate on the basis of such convictions about basic educational matters in order to give shape to his immediate decisions. This is a service rendered by his philosophy of education.

A second function of a philosophy of education relates to planning. Education is a social act in which certain persons plan prescriptive activities for other persons. Plans always reflect the planners' concept of appropriate goals and processes and involve a choice from among many possible goals and processes.[86] But the goals or processes chosen reflect some reasons for the choice, and these in turn are also chosen from among many possibilities. So that what is planned indicates that a judgment has been made, in the light of some set of standards, about what should or should not be done.

An educator has two bases for making such a judgment: either the effectiveness of an activity is measurable so that empirical evidence of success can provide the reason for choosing one process instead of another; or the effectiveness of the activity is not measurable, in which case those doing the planning must base their choices upon convictions about education and their system of values, that is, upon their philosophy of education. Since an educational activity usually is directed toward several goals at one time, the more seriously each is taken into account the more difficult it is to determine their priorities or interrelationships on the basis of measurable factors.

Even when the effectiveness of an activity is measurable, however, choices may be made in terms of philosophical commitments rather than being based upon empirical evidence of their success. For instance, statistical studies may prove that the lecture method is less efficient than laboratory experimentation in helping students to understand certain principles in physics, yet a professor may choose a less efficient teaching method because he is convinced that his lecturing will communicate the value judgments about physics which he believes are more important than measurable competencies.

Thus a philosophy of education is the principal determinant of the goals and processes incorporated in educational planning. But since each educational activity requires continuous redefinition of goal and reevaluation of process, a philosophy of education, whether explicit or implicit, continually functions as a standard for choosing among alternative goals and processes.[87]

A philosophy of education becomes functional, in a third way, in relation to the activity of conducting an educational program. Even though planning may be very inclusive and thorough there is no way to anticipate every question asked of a teacher or each problem to be faced by an administrator. Planning can at best provide only general direction for handling those factors which planners take into account. Then responsibility is transferred to teachers and administrators. If they were to carry out the plans with no regard for circumstances, they would be machines rather than teachers or administrators. Each of these professions is an art as well as a skill, and the practitioners' basic commitments always show through the practice. If an administrator is employed in a large system where functions are specialized, his own assumptions about responsibility to authority will influence his response to directives from superiors. If a teacher has no part in program-planning, his own convictions about the basic human condition will influence both the ardor with which he pursues prescribed goals and the way in which he carries out prescribed processes. A teacher's convictions about what a teacher is and ought to be, about freedom and responsibility in the classroom, about human development and the way a person learns, and about the appropriate goals of education are all operative at all times as he makes decisions moment by moment about what to do and say. Without the philosophical activity that organizes his thinking on such essential educational matters he is unable to be a responsible teacher. His philosophy of education performs an essential function as guide for interpreting and handling each step in the conduct of an educational activity.

The fourth function of a philosophy of education has already been indicated, that of evaluation. In a sense evaluation is implicit in every decision made at each step within the system of an educating process, for each decision is made within some frame of reference that reflects basic meanings and commitments. Sometimes, however, evaluation must be made from outside the process, when an administrator is assigned to a new school, when an accreditation agency sends a committee to investigate a college, or when a teacher meets a class for the first time. How the evaluation is conducted, the standards brought to bear, the kinds of questions asked, the way the findings are expressed—all of these are direct indications of the philosophical frame of reference with which the evaluator views an educational system. And the adequacy of such an evaluation is dependent upon how conscious the evaluator is of his own philosophy of education.[88]

When a school principal has to choose among prospective teachers his own educational philosophy influences his evaluation; when the new teacher plans the way he will help students understand a novel his philosophy of education influences his evaluation of how much they are able to grasp; and when a supervisor evaluates that teacher's work the supervisor's philosophy of education influences his judgments.

In none of these instances is a philosophy of education the only influential factor. Personality, appearance, facility in writing or speaking, college background, political and social convictions, aesthetic preferences, and scores of other factors may be involved, yet it is not possible to separate any of these from the views of education held by each individual. Only as one attempts to bring these views into conscious focus, to make them explicit, is it possible to identify the relationship of philosophy to practice.

The most important function performed by a philosophy of education is to provide an order by which one can think about or discuss the field. A domain as extensive as education, in its multitude of forms of expression over so many centuries in different cultures, suggests that there may be an inherent order or system that can be identified and described. The necessity of talking about education, whatever the terminology used, in each culture indicates that there is at least sufficient order to the field to generate common forms of communication within that culture. The type of language used to speak about education is itself a reflection of the way persons within a culture think about the field and the meaning it has for them. While we can assume that common discourse about education reflects deeper meanings and patterns, there is no assurance that such discourse indicates an awareness on the part of the users of that language of the philosophy they hold.

While different types of terminology may be characteristic of different cultures, when a systematic effort is made to discuss all possible views of the field with precision, as in the foundations courses of a school of education, the great variety and complexity of terminology becomes obvious. This only indicates the variety of philosophical perspectives within an advanced contemporary culture and the fact that a person's view of education is part of his general view of the world. A conscious effort to identify and clarify his own convictions and assumptions is the most basic function of philosophical activity.

ELEMENTS

While there are many different philosophies of education, the adequacy of each one depends upon whether it includes certain basic elements needed to provide a satisfactory foundation for educational theory and practice. Though an examination of these elements cannot provide a normative position on each one, "a philosophy" that does not address all the elements involved or that does not relate each to the others cannot serve the normative function of indicating the appropriate content for a philosophy of education. Six such elements are (and need to be) incorporated in every philosophy of education:

1. *A philosophy of education describes the persons toward whom educational activities may be directed.*

Education is for persons, whether particular children, a group of employees, the elderly, or all the citizens of a country. The designation of the persons who are to participate includes assumptions about their cultural situation, their educational background, their religious experiences, their intellectual capacities, and their reasons for being related to an educational activity. Such factors have to be taken into account in program-planning, but they are also implicit in a philosophy of education.

2. *A philosophy of education indicates the appropriate intentions for those participating and the reasons for such objectives.*

Since education is always an intentional activity—that is,

it is conducted by some people in order to help other people learn something—the philosophy will provide an explication of what these particular people in their situation need to study in order to learn the things intended. The intentions may be to serve national objectives, to develop particular professional competencies, or to enable a person to exercise his responsible freedom. Whatever the objectives may be, a philosophical system specifies the relation of the intentions to its basic assumptions about man. This applies whether one is developing a philosophy of vocational education, of higher education, or of humanistic education, or a position that includes all types of education. Goals are implied in each stage of an educational activity: in organizing the system or pattern, in the activities of teachers, in the participation of students, and in the kind of behavior or understanding that it is hoped a person will have after he has completed the program. It is important to examine the relation of intentions to other elements in a philosophy, because some people seem to assume that a statement of aims is a philosophy of education. More is involved, however, as is indicated in the consideration of the next four elements.

3. *A philosophy of education identifies assumptions about how the persons involved learn the things intended.*

Education always involves learning, and how persons learn is related to what they are to learn as well as to the way the mind operates. Every philosophy of education implies a learning theory that reflects basic assumptions about human nature and its relation to culture. Similarly, every educational system implies certain kinds of behavior that are appropriate for the learning process, and the extent to which the learning capacity of the student is influenced by his cultural setting and his type of personality.

4. *A philosophy of education indicates the appropriate responsibility of a teacher in helping students to learn the matters intended.*

Most learning takes place without teachers. There are many

things, however, that can be learned only with the aid of another person. The teacher may be related to the matter as an authority, a scholar, a critic, a specialist, or a translator. The teacher may be related to the student as an example, a model, an *alter* parent, a friend, a counselor, a supervisor, a judge. There are many possible teaching processes and methods available for use by teachers, but each one implies certain assumptions about the teacher's proper relationship both to the matters being studied and to the students who should be learning. The way one relates these elements in practice is an expression of his philosophy of education.

5. *A philosophy of education identifies the appropriate structures and processes that educators can employ to aid the persons involved in reaching the objectives intended.*

Since education is a social activity it inevitably requires an organizational structure and a set of typical processes. Usually these structures and processes are consciously chosen, with the choice expressing assumptions about the nature of the persons involved, the matters being considered, and the objectives intended. Yet whether consciously chosen or not, because they reflect and symbolize the intentions, structures and processes are part of the "content" of what is being taught to those who participate. The structure and processes include a vast range of aspects, such as buildings, committees for planning, administrative policies, curricular materials, administrators, specified class periods, required credits, and chalkboards. Decisions about each of these may be primarily psychological, or political, or sociological, or only traditional, yet each implies a philosophy of education.

6. *A philosophy of education relates the patterns and objectives of educational activities to the rest of the life of those involved.*

An educational philosophy recognizes that no educational activity can be isolated and self-contained. It will make explicit its understanding of the relation of these activities for these particular people to their social relations and responsibilities, and to their total understanding of life and its meaning. Whether the educational activity is narrowly specific or broadly generalized, its philosophical undergirdings identify the relation of all elements in the system to the larger social context and ultimately to its interpretation of man and the human situation. The basic position may be Marxian or Idealist, Thomist or Existentialist, but whatever the assumptions are about man and his situation, a philosophy of education identifies them and allows them to inform the views of this particular segment of reality, education.[89]

Chapter IX

EDUCATION

IN POPULAR THINKING, education is an independent reality—
"education" does things, "education" is something that acts,
"education" is an object of faith. "Education" is expected to
perform valuable social functions—to prepare one age for its
unknowable future, to prepare men and women for useful
employment, to save the state, to make men,[90] to form a generation. This way of thinking allows no occasion for examining the innumerable "pieces" making up the educational enterprise which is supposed to implement such expectations. The
moving "idea of education" held by most people is seldom a
compilation of parts; rather it is usually the product of an
image with power for social cohesion which forms the popular
conception of the field.[91] These images imply both objectives
and processes but are usually held without awareness of their
origin.

"Midwife" is one ancient image of the appropriate function
of education—to aid in bringing forth latent abilities of an
individual, to serve his capacity for development. The Latin
term *educere* has been employed to express two aspects of
this midwifery, "to educe" or "to bring out" what is already
given in human capacity.

Some think of education as an *alter* parent, and after graduation one speaks of the institution from which he has gradu-
ated as his alma mater. Education in such a view continues the

nurturing responsibilities of the family in concern for all of life, and the forming of both morals and intellect.

For others education fits into a botanical rather than a biological image, and its task is to cultivate the soil, provide fertilizer and water in order that the young plant may grow. The task is seen as planting seeds, or bending twigs,[92] and eventually bringing the harvest of fruits of the activity.

To some people education fits the image of a river, the stream of culture that sweeps along to shape the rising generation. The stream may be a flood tide that carries all before it or it may be more discriminating as it respects the personality of each student.[93]

Romantic images of disinterested seekers holding aloft the lamp of truth can be found in popular views of education. The person who fulfills such an image may be a white-coated scientist in total objective devotion to the facts wherever they may lead him—accompanied by the optimistic assumption that in this search for truth what will be found will be good.

An idyllic image of education can be seen in repeated references to the college as a sort of paradise, a place of escape from the world where in innocent retreat teachers and learners may devote themselves to academic pursuits.[94] Sometimes this is seen in negative terms, the professor as an egghead out of touch with reality and the college as an asylum for young people who are not yet ready to face life.

A more recent image of education sees it as a social adapter, as an agent of a social melting-pot function. If immigrants need to learn how to make beds, or speak English, or learn American ways, give the job to the schools. If the young need jobs or ought to know how to drive cars, education will give them the training. If the racial balance is wrong in a community, the schools are a convenient agency for correcting the situation. The schools are seen as agents of social change.[95]

Education for most people is identified with schooling, and a pervasive contemporary image of schools is that of a factory available to produce whatever society requires.[96] Few would go so far as to claim that all graduates should be identical in competency, but the standardization of both admissions and graduation requirements is a long step toward such a model. The university is particularly subject to this image and many students assume that when they pay tuition fees they are purchasing a product of the educational factory.

Each of these images has had the power to move many people, to attract loyalty, to encourage the endowment of vast institutions committed to one or another image, to persuade societies to devote a large share of their resources to conducting educational enterprises based on a particular image. Each image, however, by being so all-inclusive, by focusing only on long-range goals, oversimplifies both the goals and the processes of education and makes claims for education that cannot be redeemed. For each image there are "true believers" [97] who are either unwilling or unable to examine critically the gap between the implications of the image to which they are committed and the reality by which their commitment is expressed. Such images are powerful on the unconscious level and may be clearly seen in educational architecture. A building committee and their architect may not realize that their selection of a site and the design of a campus are profoundly influenced by the assumption that "of course" a college should be an idyllic escape from the world. Or the school board and architect may never realize that the high school building is designed, and looks, like a factory. Such unconscious commitments also find expression in popular verbalization at commencement addresses. It is much more difficult to express these images in the processes of an educational program, for their goals are so broad as to be unmeasurable, and if they cannot be measured, the results of the educational system cannot guide the design or planning of that system.

The identification of the formative images that shape social concerns for education is but another way of indicating that education is always an integral part of a larger cultural whole. The study of any educational program or structure can be adequate only when it gives attention to the many threads that tie it into the web of its cultural setting.[98]

It is necessary to examine part by part the many interrelated aspects of the educational phenomenon in order to understand what actually goes on. This has been the preoccupation of the previous eight chapters. Definitions of education may be comparatively easy when attempting to express an enveloping image, but a definition that discriminates for each of the essential elements in an educational enterprise is less easy to compose and has less power to move people. Such a definition,[99] therefore, is intended to aid the person who, either as a professional or as a layman, seeks to understand what education is in reality, in order to make responsible educational decisions. Such a definition begins with description.

Of course description does not in itself protect from narrowness. The term "education" applies to so many types of activities that different definitions are often mutually exclusive. The most frequent use is *institutional-descriptive* in reference to schools that are set up with a conscious aim of conducting a process called education. Nearly as frequently the term is applied to *content-acquisition* as in the phrase "he got an education." Sometimes this usage is extended to imply a general *normative-standard* to distinguish between learning which is or is not considered adequate or appropriate. At other times "education" is used in a particularly *moral-behavioral* sense with emphasis upon the type of conduct produced by the schooling process. Some uses of the term are more definitive in expressing a particular *epistemological position* on the assumption that only knowledge of a particular kind can be "education." The least common use of "education" is as an *inclusive-descriptive* term referring to the total phenomenon in all its forms and concepts.

Implicit in all description is the identification of what is being described. Throughout the analysis of education in the preceding chapters it has been necessary to delimit areas for consideration. A definition of "education" can be helpful for responsible educators only as it specifies and discriminates its areas of applicability.

Significant discussion of education is seriously hampered by its indeterminate meaning. "Education," if it is to be a word with communicative value, and particularly if it is to provide a conceptually delimited area for disciplined study and activity,[100] needs to be less inclusive. Particularly when definitions are expected to provide a basis for theory and practice they need to be as precise as possible.

Developing educational theories and programs, and evaluating them, raises for every educator a basic problem, How is it possible to take all relevant factors into account? Theoretically, at least in a formal way, it might be possible to computerize all possible categories of every range, but it is not possible to "read" the developing interrelationships, moment by moment, in any individual or to divide the possible influence these will have upon the next moment of learning.

No matter how carefully planned an educational activity may be, it is never possible to anticipate all the consequences of that activity. Educational planners may set up vocational schools to train more dressmakers or metalworkers, but they cannot control the number of young people who marry because they met in those schools, or how many go into the intended occupations, or the new ideas each student accepted during the courses. Only later studies can document the influence of such courses on the lives of the students, or catalog what they "learned."

So, a definition of education can give direction for developing relevant theories or programs only when it is based on a realistic account of what takes place in the educational process.

A Descriptive Definition

EDUCATION IS A CONSCIOUSLY SELECTED SET OF ACTIVITIES . . . Though a variety of specific actions is involved in each step of an educational occasion, such as speaking, location, group arrangement, etc., education incorporates a set of these consciously[101] placed in relation to each other for some purpose. Unconscious learning provides the major channel for cultural adaptation and transmission, and unconscious learning must be assumed as part of the setting within which planned activities take place, but because the activities are planned they are consciously selected from among many possibilities.

. . . IN WHICH AN INDIVIDUAL OR A GROUP INTENTIONALLY . . . The intentionality of education is primarily that of the individuals or groups planning and presenting educational activities for others. A school may be the idea of one individual, yet its program is the product of the administration and teachers, and perhaps of parents, all of whom hold a variety of intentions—that is, expectations, hopes, images, and standards for what the school ought to do. Education implies cooperation among individuals with their various intentions who have adopted a procedure by which they can agree on what is to be done, plan for, and present it.

. . . PRESENTS SELECTED IDEAS OR ACTIONS . . . Education involves initiation on the part of those conducting the educational program, and the initiation involves some matter to be thought about or considered. The subject matter of education may include all ranges of learning, but those conducting the activity select from limitless possibilities the content that is germane to this particular occasion.

. . . TO PARTICULAR INDIVIDUALS . . . Education, as a conscious, intentional, planned activity, is adapted to the persons toward whom the activity is directed. The individuals to be involved in any activity thus have a "claim" upon teachers or sponsors to take their situation and capacities into account. Every educational activity thus is particular, and the circumstances of the "teacher" and of the learners shape both the matter that needs to be presented as well as the processes employed.

. . . IN A PARTICULAR SETTING . . . All education is particular, also, in its physical, geographical, cultural, and temporal setting. Every factor in the surrounding circumstances influences motivation, structures, and processes. Programs designed for middle-class suburban schools cannot be the same, nor can they produce the same responses, in schools in poverty-ridden slums.

. . . BY A CONTROLLED PROCESS . . . Education implies that the process employed is as much a concern as are the ideas or behavior being presented, because the two cannot be separated. The process may be simple or very elaborate, may involve only a few people or very many. The process incorporates some measurements or testing to provide a basis for future planning.

. . . THAT SEEKS THE STUDENT'S UNDERSTANDING . . . The point of the process is that the student shall understand the ideas or actions being presented. One of the qualifications, therefore, in considering the particular individuals toward whom the program is directed, is their level of comprehension, their ability to understand the ideas and actions being considered.

. . . AND HIS CONSCIOUS CHOICE OF RESPONSE. The learning that takes place in the educational process is in the response by the student to whatever is presented and to the setting in which the educational occasion takes place. Part of that setting is internal, so the student responds in terms of his prior experience and his interpretation of that experience. This means that a student always brings with him to an educational occasion some interpretation of what is to be learned; thus all education is reeducation. There is always response, but education implies that the student is conscious of his own response and thus is able to articulate it, either in words or in action, with an understanding of what he is doing and saying. Freedom is essential to this response. A social system may establish controls over what is said or done, but underneath the controls, in the inner response to his situation, the student is free. His response cannot be prescribed.

So—EDUCATION IS A CONSCIOUSLY SELECTED SET OF ACTIVITIES

IN WHICH AN INDIVIDUAL OR A GROUP INTENTIONALLY PRESENTS SELECTED IDEAS OR ACTIONS TO PARTICULAR INDIVIDUALS IN A PARTICULAR SETTING BY A CONTROLLED PROCESS THAT SEEKS THE STUDENT'S UNDERSTANDING AND HIS CONSCIOUS CHOICE OF RESPONSE.

Because every element in an educational activity is in constant flux (group intentions, the matter being presented, the students, the available processes, the interpretation of understanding, the possible responses) the educator may view his responsibility as a series of strategic decisions in which he attempts to take into account all relevant factors.

DEFINITION AS NORM

Such a descriptive definition of education may also be employed normatively,[102] that is, it may be used to determine from the perspective of one who holds such a view what is or is not education. From this point of view one-step teaching-learning activities, that is, when an idea is presented for acceptance, may be training or indoctrination but they are not education. Programs on radio or television that are presented without the possibility of identifying who is listening or how they respond may be compared with selling or promoting, but they are not education. A TV commercial presents ideas and recommends actions, but education requires feedback from the learner in order to discern what is learned, and the number of cars or bottles of perfume sold is not a discriminating indicator of the total response of listeners. Such use of mass media does not require the seller to have concern for the particular individual who may be listening. His concern is for the sale of cars or perfume.

A distressing handicap for many educators is the popular assumption that education is really only a set of methods and tools, which can be quickly learned, which bear no philosophical implications, and which work alike for all kinds of subject matter. Those who view education in this way see it as a set of tools, a piece of machinery, and the educator as an impersonal operator. Their only question is of the goal on the assumption that when the goal is decided—the mold installed —the machine can go into operation and stamp out the products. But this is not education. Every process expresses a world view about man and his nature; it also expresses a philosophy of education. Therefore, no process is neutral and no true educator is just a mechanic.

The most frequent popular distinction between types of education is by age or by subject matter—elementary, secondary and graduate or medical education, legal education, theological education—which usually implies that "education" has a common meaning for each field. This is another expression of the assumption that content and method are independent, and that education can be seen as a set of methods that bear no distinctive content. But that is not education.

A "controlled" process does not mean that the outcome is controlled but that the process has a theoretical base which is an attempt to understand human behavior and that the processes of the educational program are informed by that theory. Thus the methods, procedures, facilities, and settings are recognized as important in the learning process; but they may be used in such a way that the student is only expected to accept rather than to understand. Response without understanding is conditioning, not education, nor is a process that expects response that is not free even when understood. This is not to deny that often teaching goes on in business or in the army when great care is given so that a matter is thoroughly understood but the learner does not have a choice as to his particular reasons. This is training, but not education.

From the perspective of the definition presented above education cannot be equated with "learning." Learning may take place in front of a television set during a commercial, but that is not education. Learning may take place while a person reads an impressive public relations brochure trying to get him to contribute to his alma mater, but that is not education.

Nor are indoctrination and brainwashing education. Thus the definition may be employed as a norm to determine what is not education.

In the same way this definition can serve as a norm to be employed in designing new programs that are "education" or for evaluating existing patterns and programs. As such it should aid the educator to be aware of the many dimensions of the field and to be sensitive to their interaction. This understanding of education helps an educator to develop a comprehensive view. It should normally be his responsibility to struggle to see most clearly the larger frame of reference within which the educational activity is conducted, to be an interpreter of the historical setting, the philosophical framework, and the elements essential to good education. No one can pretend to be an expert on every aspect of life, but he should attempt to expose himself, to be sensitized, to the many elements that influence self-understanding, and to help others to be similarly sensitized. These are essential to effective education.

The educator should recognize that he will always be dealing with more elements than he can control or fully comprehend, so he must both act upon what is known and develop procedures for further research in openness toward future findings that may call for changed structures and processes of social activity. The thousand threads of a student's life bear multitudes of dynamics that cannot be synchronized to what the educator would like to do. So he either decides to organize what he will do with his resources as a responsible person or he puts himself in neutral and goes where he is pushed.

Amid the complex tensions of each educational occasion, an educator must develop the ability to articulate the issues involved for an individual or for a group. Significant reinterpreting and restructuring depends upon clarity. One may know many teaching methods and develop imaginative creative skills, but if he does not know how to analyze the situation that might call for such skills, they are useless. The educator is not just an arranger, an enabler, a precipitator, an instigator, or a promoter. His special concern should be to develop the capacity to clarify the issues being faced by an individual or a group or a community and to assist others in such clarification. When education is approached functionally and understood in the light of its many dimensions and processes, a more fruitful setting is provided for the examination of its popular images and the effective relation of philosophy to practice.

The conscientious practitioner of education—whether parent, school principal, classroom teacher, university president, foreman in a factory, or business administrator—recognizes that he or she is under pressure from three directions. The relative response given to each of these pressures largely determines the shape and direction of the education each conducts.

One pressure is the expectation of the social groups directly involved—community, teachers, parents, and students. Their ideas of what constitutes education, the functions they think are appropriate for an educational activity, and their own desires, prejudices, and selfishness—all of these reflect in the pressure of their expectations.

A second pressure is the inertia of past patterns expressed in institutionalism, the design of buildings, the dependency of many individuals upon the way things have been done.

Each of these pressures reflect a third—the implicit philosophies of education held by all the people involved. Seldom are these philosophies articulated—they are assumed. They may be collections of ideas about details or comprehensive sets of principles, yet they inform both the expectations and the inertia.

Educational strategy, therefore, can be adequate only when it takes these pressures into account and responds to the dynamics of its situation. Education is always a series of strategic decisions which, while grounded upon a realistic appraisal of its situation and built upon existing dynamics, reaches toward a more inclusive perspective for understanding our existence and responsible decision-making.

REFERENCES—QUOTATIONS—COMMENTS

1. I was a consultant conducting a self-evaluation by the faculty members of the Facultad Evangelica de Teologia, in Buenos Aires, Argentina.

2. "Once observations are turned into theories a blindness sets in for the phenomena not represented in the theories." (Roger Brown, "Transcultural Studies in Cognition," in *American Anthropologist*, Special Issue, 1964, p. 250.)

3. John Walton and James L. Kuethe (eds.), *The Discipline of Education* (University of Wisconsin Press, 1963). This book is a collection of papers presented at a summer conference on this theme conducted at Johns Hopkins University.

4. Marc Belth, *Education as a Discipline* (Allyn and Bacon, Inc., 1965).

5. In a small book, *An Introduction to the Analysis of Educational Concepts* (Addison-Wesley Publishing Company, Inc., 1968), Jonas F. Soltis attempts "to introduce anyone without a background in philosophy to a new way of approaching and examining quite ordinary yet central ideas which are fundamental to the everyday business of educating" (p. iii). The first five chapters of the book illustrate the analytic approach to such concepts as subject matter, knowledge, teaching, learning, and understanding. The sixth chapter, "Epilogue," offers a very helpful annotated bibliography of the analytic literature that has stirred wide interest and participation in England and the United States. Soltis describes the contribution of analysis as follows: "It is my firm belief that one of the greatest advantages to the use of analysis in education is just this proximity of the types of problems and ideas dealt with to the down-to-earth, everyday business of educating. Moreover, the impatient attitude of the analytic philosopher toward fuzzy thinking and vague ideas,

should it be caught by many practicing educators, could prove to be the single most important contribution of philosophy of education to educational practice today. . . . To make the language of education work, we must be clear about its intent and meaning and not be swayed only by its imagery and poetry. The analytic temperament and techniques should prove most useful to any practicing educator in getting him to think through with care and precision just what it is he is buying from theorists, and, more importantly, just what it is that he is after and how best that might be achieved. As I have pointed out elsewhere, much of what goes on in good teaching occurs in the mind of the teacher long before he or she enters the classroom. It is precisely this 'thinking through' process that the techniques and results of analysis have most to offer the practicing educator." (Pp. 73 f.)

6. Walter Kerr has provided an interesting parallel in the attempt to understand the contemporary theater. Writing in *The New York Times Magazine*, Sept. 1, 1968, under the title of "The Theater of Say It! Show It! What Is It?" he suggests that contemporary dramatists are no longer satisfied with plays that carefully exclude "the gratuitous and the irrelevant." He writes: "In our new state of mind we distrust what is orderly because we are now sharply aware that in everything ordered there is something extremely arbitrary. To have an order of any kind—political, religious, social, domestic—some of the things embraced must be arbitrarily embraced, whether they quite suit us or not; some of the things excluded must be arbitrarily excluded. We are terribly conscious—at this moment in time—of the fact that we do not really conform well to the roles and systems we have ourselves adopted. In shaping the roles and systems, too much of us was left out. We don't fit and we know it. . . . Though the entire world is obviously and often violently engaged in the process of forcing all patterns open to see what has gone into their making—and what has failed to go into their making that ought to have been there—the mood is not truly despairing. It is determined. All of us must see more, hear more, risk more, embrace more if we are to understand the bad fit and perhaps get a better one.

"And so our heads swivel for a closer look. Above all, for a more inclusive look—without predisposition, without automatic exclusion of any kind, without *selection*. If we are going to select beforehand, we shall miss the same things we missed last time. Indeed, if any principle of selection is to function at all, it must be the principle of selecting now what was never selected before. *Nothing* can be called irrelevant if we are trying to find out what relevance is.

"Thus the theater, like everything else in life, comes under two commands and a question. Say it. Show it. What is it?" (Pp. 11, 14.)

Mr. Kerr employs current Broadway productions to illustrate his thesis, and concludes the article with these observations: "If I had to sum up the whole business in the fastest conceivable way, I'd simply say that we have moved from a logical theater into a phenomenological one. Look at the thing hard. What thing? Everything. And don't try to say what it is until you've had it long enough in hand to know its tricks. Shape will come again. Now what about *shapes?*" (P. 21.)

7. Joseph J. Kockelmans (ed.), *Phenomenology: The Philosophy of Edmund Husserl and Its Interpretation* (Doubleday & Company, Inc., 1967).

8. *Ibid.,* p. 5.

9. Among the major works about phenomenology and by leading phenomenologists are:

INTRODUCTIONS

Kockelmans, Joseph J. (ed.), *Phenomenology: The Philosophy of Edmund Husserl and Its Interpretation.* Doubleday & Company, Inc., 1967.

Spiegelberg, Herbert, *The Phenomenological Movement: A Historical Introduction.* The Hague: Martinus Nijhoff, 1960. 2 vols.

Strasser, Stephan, *Phenomenology and the Human Sciences.* Duquesne University Press, 1963.

BY HUSSERL

Cartesian Meditations: An Introduction to Phenomenology. Humanities Press, Inc., 1960.

Phenomenology and the Crisis of Philosophy. Harper & Row, Publishers, Inc., 1965.

Ideas. Collier Book. The Macmillan Company, 1967.

The Phenomenology of Internal Time-Consciousness. Indiana University Press, 1967.

ABOUT HUSSERL

Farber, M., *The Foundation of Phenomenology: Edmund Husserl and the Quest for a Rigorous Science of Philosophy.* Harvard University Press, 1943.

Lauer, Quentin, *Edmund Husserl: Phenomenology and the Crisis of Philosophy.* Harper & Row, Publishers, Inc., 1965.

Welch, E. Parl, *The Philosophy of Edmund Husserl: The Origin and Development of His Phenomenology.* Columbia University Press, 1965.

By Heidegger

Being and Time. Harper & Row, Publishers, Inc., 1962.
Question of Being. College and University Press Services, Inc., 1964.
Discourse on Thinking. Harper & Row, Publishers, Inc., 1966.
What Is a Thing? Henry Regnery Company, 1966.

About Heidegger

Langan, Thomas, *The Meaning of Heidegger: A Critical Study of an Existentialist Phenomenology.* Columbia University Press, 1959.
Richardson, William J., *Heidegger: Through Phenomenology to Thought.* The Hague: Martinus Nijhoff, 1963.
Vycinas, Vincent, *Earth and Gods: An Introduction to the Philosophy of Martin Heidegger.* The Hague: Martinus Nijhoff, 1961.

By Merleau-Ponty

The Phenomenology of Perception. Humanities Press, Inc., 1963.
Structures of Behavior. Beacon Press, Inc., 1963.
Sense and Non-Sense. Northwestern University Press, 1964.
Signs. Northwestern University Press, 1964.

About Merleau-Ponty

Barral, Mary Rose, *Merleau-Ponty: The Role of the Body-Subject in Interpersonal Relations.* Duquesne University Press, 1965.
Kwant, Remy C., *The Phenomenological Philosophy of Merleau-Ponty.* Duquesne University Press, 1963.
Langan, Thomas, *Merleau-Ponty's Critique of Reason.* Yale University Press, 1966.

By Ricoeur

Fallible Man. Henry Regnery Company, 1965.
History and Truth. Northwestern University Press, 1965.
Freedom and Nature: The Voluntary and the Involuntary. Northwestern University Press, 1966.
Symbolism of Evil. Harper & Row, Publishers, Inc., 1967.

10. Martin Heidegger, *Being and Time,* tr. by John Macquarrie and Edward Robinson (London: SCM Press, Ltd., 1962), pp. 46 f.

11. The fact that Merleau-Ponty describes phenomenology some-

what differently indicates something of the range of views among phenomenological philosophers. He writes: "What is phenomenology? It may seem strange that this question has still to be asked half a century after the first works of Husserl. The fact remains that it has by no means been answered. Phenomenology is the study of essences; and according to it, all problems amount to finding definitions of essences: the essence of perception, or the essence of consciousness, for example. But phenomenology is also a philosophy which puts essences back into existence, and does not expect to arrive at an understanding of man and the world from any starting point other than that of their 'facticity.' It is a transcendental philosophy which places in abeyance the assertions arising out of the natural attitude, the better to understand them; but it is also a philosophy for which the world is always 'already there' before reflection begins—as an inalienable presence; and all its efforts are concentrated upon re-achieving a direct and primitive contact with the world, and endowing that contact with a philosophical status. It is the search for a philosophy which shall be a 'rigorous science,' but it also offers an account of space-time and the world as we 'live' them. It tries to give a direct description of our experience as it is, without taking account of its psychological origin and the causal explanations which the scientist, the historian or the sociologist may be able to provide." (*The Phenomenology of Perception*, tr. by Colin Smith, p. vii; London: Routledge & Kegan Paul, Ltd., 1962.)

12. Ernst Kreick, *Grundiss der Erziehungs-wissenschaft* (Leipzig: Quelle and Meyer, 1927).

13. While "comparative education" has developed as a significant field in some universities and schools of education, most of the writing in the field has focused upon the structures, programs, and methodologies of education in other countries while relatively little attention has been given to more basic aspects of developing philosophy and theory. The following books attempt to examine the latter aspects. Vernon Mallinson's *An Introduction to the Study of Comparative Education* (London: William Heinemann, Ltd., 1960) is limited to European schools and relates educational patterns to "national character." Prof. Nicholas Hans traces the relation of types of education in Europe and America to the major factors of religion and social philosophy in *Comparative Education: A Study of Educational Factors and Traditions* (London: Routledge & Kegan Paul, Ltd., 1949). See also Brian Holmes's *Problems in Education: A Comparative Approach* (London: Routledge & Kegan Paul, Ltd., 1965).

14. Analytic philosophers are equally careful to maintain their

neutrality, for it would be fruitless to attempt to examine the uses of words, concepts, and metaphors on the assumption that their normative use is the objective of the analysis. "In this introduction to the analysis of educational concepts, we generally have avoided questions of value and, in fact, have attempted to act neutrally with respect to commitments to value positions. I have already indicated that this is not to deny the close connection between education and value judgments, for I do agree with Peters that educating does involve questions of value in a very important way. But while this is so, one of the strengths of the neutral stance of analysis is its potential to provide a methodological means to hold our own values at bay while we search into the logical features of educational ideas. In this way, the techniques employed by the analytic philosopher resemble the *value-neutral* techniques of the social scientist, who attempts thereby to control his inquiry and produce results which are objective in the sense that others who may hold different values still may agree with the results obtained." (Soltis, *An Introduction to the Analysis of Educational Concepts*, p. 68.)

15. "Genuine seeing—not just staring, which is not genuine seeing—always takes place within the structure of figure and horizon, and this figure implies an organization of the visible world. The field of our seeing is the world. In this world there are concealed an indefinite number of visible objects, but these objects are only latently visible, potentially visible. To become visible in the genuine sense of the term, they must rise up as figures against the horizon of the world. But they will do this only when man, as meaning-giving existence, assigns a meaning to them. Man makes something arise as a figure from the horizon of the world, as he gives meaning to it and thereby organizes the world. If a primitive man is suddenly transplanted into a large modern city, many objects in this city remain invisible to him. Note that we do not say: 'There are many things which he does not see,' but 'Many things remain invisible to him.' His existence as giver of meaning has not developed to the point where he is able to raise these things as figures from the horizon of the world. For this reason we have said above that these things are only 'potentially visible.'" (Remy C. Kwant, *Phenomenology of Social Existence*, p. 70; Duquesne University Press, 1965.)

16. "No practical problem is solved merely by analysing it. Analysis is meant to bring a situation . . . within the grasp of human reason—formulas, rationalizations, conceptualizations, tools to gain insight. . . . Analysis continually establishes the Gordian knot." (C. A. O. van Nieuwenhuijze, *Cross Cultural Studies*, p. 64; The Hague: Mouton & Co., 1963.)

17. Ernst Cassirer has given special attention to the place of symbolism in man's cultural development. In *An Essay on Man: An Introduction to a Philosophy of Human Culture* (Doubleday & Company, Inc., 1953), he writes: "Between the receptor system and the effector system, which is to be found in all animal species, we find in man a third link which we may describe as the symbolic system. This new acquisition transforms the whole of human life. As compared with the other animals man lives not merely in a broader reality; he lives, so to speak, in a new *dimension* of reality." (Pp. 42 f.) "Reason is a very inadequate term with which to comprehend the forms of man's cultural life in all their richness and variety. But all these forms are symbolic forms. Hence, instead of defining man as an *animal rationale,* we should define him as an *animal symbolicum.* . . . But it now becomes imperative that we develop this definition somewhat in order to give it greater precision. That symbolic thought and symbolic behavior are among the most characteristic features of human life, and that the whole progress of human culture is based on these conditions, is undeniable." (Pp. 44 f.)

18. Another way to view the "settings" of speech is in terms of their functions within a culture. Dell H. Hymes has suggested four of these: (*a*) in terms of the materials of speech, there is the patterning of utterances in discourse; (*b*) in terms of individual participants, there is patterning of expression and interpretation of personality; (*c*) in terms of the social system, there is the patterning of speech situations; and (*d*) in terms of cultural values and outlooks, there is the patterning of attitudes and conceptions of speech. ("Functions of Speech: An Evolutionary Approach," in *Anthropology and Education,* The Martin G. Brumbaugh Lectures on Education, ed. by F. C. Gruber; University of Pennsylvania Press, 1961.)

19. While attempts are not being made at this point to examine the mental processes by which a person comes to understand and use language, it is important to realize that language is the tool by which a person understands. He does not first understand and then formulate the understanding linguistically. Emmanuel G. Mesthene offers an illuminating interpretation of John Dewey's thinking on this point. In *Logic,* Dewey had asserted that it is by means of discourse that an indeterminate situation is made into a determinate one. Mesthene contends that "the main conclusion of Dewey's *Logic* is that the process of getting knowledge and the process of putting that knowledge into language are the same process. That is, inquiry and formulation are identical; they are one process, not two. . . . The two aspects are indeed distinguishable, but they

are not two separate processes" (p. 513). "Language is the agent of actualization; that is why it makes us know. Language can do that because of a peculiarity of its own structure. Whereas natural structures are potential in existence, the structure of language is potential in its axioms, which generally don't have any direct correlation with existential structures. Language is therefore free to juggle and examine any structures whatever, provided only that they are not contradictory. The structures that discourse deals with only have to be possible; they don't have to reflect structures that are present in nature, even potentially." See *Logic*, John Dewey, pp. 394 f. (Emmanuel G. Mesthene, "The Role of Language in the Philosophy of John Dewey," in "Philosophy and Phenomenological Research," *Journal of the International Phenomenological Society*, Vol. XIX, June, 1959, pp. 513, 516; University of Buffalo.)

20. Ps. 73:3.

21. The term "ideological" first gained currency in the attack of Marxists upon the capitalists who, they contended, used ideas as screens for vested interests thus making the ideas invalid. In addition they objected to the assumption that ideas are determining forces in themselves in political and economic affairs; Marx and Engels saw ideas as "echoes" of the more basic "material" causes. Such a narrow use of the term is no longer justified, in part because even Marxists can see that Marxian ideas are as subject to this charge as are the ideas of others.

In the first chapter of a collection of passages from the writings of nineteenth-century philosophers, titled *The Age of Ideology* (The New American Library of World Literature, Inc., 1956), the editor, Henry D. Aiken, recounts the shifting meaning of the term "ideology," including this description of Marxian usage: "There are several features of Marx and Engels' conception of ideology which require some mention here. In the first place, what they call 'ideology' includes not only the theory of knowledge and politics, but also metaphysics, ethics, religion, and indeed any 'form of consciousness' which expresses the basic attitudes or commitments of a social class. . . . The associations of irrationality and of ulterior social or political interest which are still frequently attached to 'ideological' doctrines have many of their roots in the Marxian theory that the ideological, and hence philosophical, components of consciousness belong exclusively to the 'superstructure' of culture. . . . In fact, according to Marx, ideologies are merely 'reflexes' or 'echoes' of other determining forces that do the fundamental work in bringing about any real social change. Marx calls such executive or efficient causes of social change 'material,' and he does so to contrast them with their ideological by-products.

"This is not the place to undertake a full-dress analysis or appraisal of Marx and Engels' not always consistent statements about the relations between the ideological superstructure and its material economic foundation. But the suggestion is always implicit in their theory that ideological doctrines are social myths or 'opiates' of the people, and that the 'reasons' for their acceptance have, at bottom, nothing to do with considerations of evidence or fact. This suggestion clings to the concept of ideology to this day." (Pp. 17–19.)

For further reading about "ideology," see:

Corbett, Patrick, *Ideologies*. Harcourt, Brace and World, Inc., 1966.

Lerner, Max, *Ideas Are Weapons: The History and Use of Ideas*. The Viking Press, Inc., 1939.

Mannheim, Karl, *Ideology and Utopia: An Introduction to the Sociology of Knowledge*. London: Kegan Paul, Trench, Trubner & Co., Ltd., 1936.

Whitehead, Alfred North, *Adventures of Ideas*. The Macmillan Company, 1933.

22. Kenneth Boulding, in *The Meaning of the 20th Century* (Harper & Row, Publishers, Inc., 1964), uses the word "ideology" in the more general frame of reference which is employed here: "An ideology may be defined as that part of his image of the world which a person defines as essential to his identity or his image of himself. . . . His ideology, therefore, is a part of a man's image of the world which is peculiarly valuable to him and which he is concerned to defend and propagate." (P. 159.) "The first essential characteristic of an ideology is then an interpretation of history sufficiently dramatic and convincing so that the individual feels he can identify with it and which in turn can give the individual a role in the drama it portrays." (P. 162.)

23. Such occasions were the failure of Nazism in Germany, of Emperor worship in Japan, and of Communism for the authors of *The God That Failed*, ed. by Richard Crossman (Harper & Brothers, 1949).

24. "This essentially cumulative irreversible character of learning things is the hallmark of science." (J. Robert Oppenheimer, in an interview on "Science and Culture," *Americas*, November, 1961, p. 3.)

25. Howard S. Becker, writing on "The Nature of a Profession,"

in *Education for the Professions,* The Sixty-first Yearbook of the
National Society for the Study of Education, Part II, ed. by
Nelson B. Henry (The University of Chicago Press, 1962), describes two competing concepts of a profession—the scientific and
the moral-evaluative. Since the difference between the two cannot
be resolved he suggests that the term should be used as "an hon-
orific symbol in our society." He goes on to write: "Professions as
commonly conceived are occupations which possess a monopoly of
some esoteric and difficult body of knowledge. Further, this knowledge is considered to be necessary for the continued functioning
of the society. What the members of the profession know and can
do is tremendously important, but no one else knows or can do
these things. . . . The body of knowledge over which the profession holds a monopoly consists not in technical skill and the
fruits of practical experience but, rather, of abstract principles arrived at by scientific research and logical analysis. This knowledge
cannot be applied routinely but must be applied wisely and judi-
ciously to each case." (P. 34.) "The symbol of the profession, however, portrays a group whose members have altruistic motivations
and whose professional activities are governed by a code of ethics
which heavily emphasizes devotion to service for the good of the
client, and condemns misuse of professional skills for selfish
purposes. This code of ethics, furthermore, is sternly enforced by
appropriate disciplinary bodies. Professional associations have as
their major purpose the enforcement of such ethical codes." (P.
36.) All of this is part of the symbol. Becker concludes his chapter
by observing that "professional education tends to build curricula
and programs in ways suggested by the symbol and so fails to prepare its students for the world they will have to work in." (P. 45.)

26. Naum Gabo offers a particularly interesting definition of
"art." "I denominate by the word art the specific and exclusive
faculty of man's mind to conceive and represent the world without
and within him in form and by means of artfully constructed images. Moreover, I maintain that this faculty predominates in all
the processes of our mental and physical orientation in this world,
it being impossible for our minds to perceive or arrange or act
upon our world in any other way but through this construction of
an ever-changing and yet coherent chain of images. Furthermore,
I maintain that these mentally constructed images are the very
essence of the reality of the world which we are searching for."
("On Constructive Realism," in Katherine S. Dreier, James Johnson Sweeney, and Naum Gabo, *Three Lectures on Modern Art,*
p. 70; Philosophical Library, Inc., 1950.)

27. C. P. Snow has made a passionate appeal for everyone to understand contemporary scientific developments, in *The Two Cultures and the Scientific Revolution* (London: Cambridge University Press, 1959).

28. Ellis Nelson provides an illuminating description of how a person builds his interpretation of reality. He writes: "Events are bits of reality. We have already defined reality as that to which a person responds, but reality imposes itself on us in small pieces. Life is like a moving picture. The film in a movie is a series of still pictures which, when shown in succession, give the impression of motion. Events are something like that. They are specific. They occur in a definite time and place even if they continue for weeks or months. They are unique. Events happen a certain way and will not be repeated that same way again. Events are rather well-defined although one event may impinge on another or blend into another. However, the event has a unity to it which makes it separate enough to report, analyse, and remember. Stringing events together gives us the sense of motion in our life; and some events, like some scenes in a movie, are decisive ones for many of the smaller ordinary events that follow.

"Because events are bits of reality, they usually involve conflict. At this point they form a close association with drama. A play would be scarcely worth seeing (indeed, would it be a play at all?) if it did not have conflict between characters, within a person, or between causes to which one might give himself. To see unrelated actions, words, or living conditions on the stage would have no significance. An event has a multitude of parts, but they are related; they are also in conflict, because each human being involved is trying to shape the parts to fit his convenience or his will. If he were not so energized, he would not be dealing with what he thinks is real. Matters on which we readily compromise or about which we argue little are matters that do not fundamentally affect our understanding of reality. We can probably say that the closer we get to reality, the sharper will be our conflicts. . . . Learning takes place according to a person's participation in events and is conditioned by his awareness of what is happening, by his personal characteristics and abilities and by the perceptual system that has been built into him by his culture." (*Where Faith Begins*, pp. 92 f.; John Knox Press, 1967.)

29. Dewey made a helpful distinction, in the idea of "experience," between the active and passive elements. The passive is "undergoing" while the active element is "trying." He wrote in *Democracy and Education* (The Macmillan Company, 1925):

"To 'learn from experience' is to make a backward and forward connection between what we do to things and what we enjoy or suffer from things in consequence. Under such conditions, doing becomes a trying; an experiment with the world to find out what it is like; the undergoing becomes instruction—discovery of the connection of things.

"Two conclusions important for education follow. (1) Experience is primarily an active-passive affair; it is not primarily cognitive. But (2) the *measure of the value* of an experience lies in the perception of relationships or continuities to which it leads up." (P. 164.)

Dewey was firm in his refusal to separate the cognitive from experience yet such a separation is often made, as James E. Russell makes, in *Change and Challenge in American Education* (Houghton Mifflin Company, 1965), when he writes: "We will need to make it our main objective to develop the abstract rational powers, and to learn how to do it so as to free the minds of mature persons from the limitations of experience. The alternative is to condemn a significant share of the American people to drudgery, or slavery, or both." (P. 24.)

30. H. G. Barrett has made a significant examination of *Innovation: The Basis of Cultural Change* (McGraw-Hill Book Company, Inc., 1953), in an effort to trace the sources of new patterns and ideas in a culture. He observes the relation of interpretation of experience to creativity, and concludes with these words: "The questions of when past experience does bear upon perception and what its effects are lead us to the heart of the problem of innovation. It appears that previous experience structures subsequent perception more often than the principal protagonists of gestalt theory have been willing to allow. It also appears that the ordering of a present sensory report in terms of some past experience like it can be more creative than is generally recognized. The mental interaction between what is and what was, in fact, does provide the only basis for a recombination of natural events; that is, for innovation, the uniquely mental contribution to newness." (P. 448.)

31. Charles J. Brauner introduced the descriptive phrase, "the map in the background," in an essay included in *Philosophy of Education: Essays and Commentaries*, ed. by Hobert W. Burns (The Ronald Press Co., 1962). "Cultural anthropologists have pointed out that a given way of classifying nature influences what an observer will see and how he will wonder about what he has seen. Linguists demonstrate that a given language influences the

ways in which one organizes his experiences, and how one reasons about his experience is conditioned by the grammar he uses. Psychologists indicate that one generally perceives what he expects to perceive, and that these perceptual sets influence behavior, for perception is the prelude to action. Sociologists report that social pressures subtly yet perceptibly dictate the range of human experiences open to men and thus influence the kinds of experience men seek or avoid.

"Such maps in the background cannot be ignored; they guide the human adventure. For instance, the Hopi Indian who believes that the ritual rain dance will influence the coming of the rain relies on a map in the background that is unreadable by most of us. . . .

"Even in providing a map based on factual information and verifiable theory, science itself requires a map of its own to guide the exploration of the unknown; in a certain strange sense a map of the unknown is needed before the unknown can be explored— or, at least, tools appropriate to the exploration are required. These useful tools, the method and language of science, themselves have a map already built into them, and this map in the background influences *how* men will wonder as well as *what* they will wonder about. What men know or believe, or think they know or believe, directs what they look for; and what they look for largely determines what they are likely to find. That which is accepted as making sense sets a precedent for what will be accepted as sensible thereafter, and what is not roughed in on the map in the background is not likely to be drawn in on the map in the foreground." (Pp. 4 ff.)

32. As in Toynbee's analysis of the rise and fall of civilizations depending upon their response to the challenges to their existence. See Arnold J. Toynbee, *A Study of History* (London: Oxford University Press, 1934). In the 1951 edition, Vol. I, Pt. II, see the section on "Challenge and Response," pp. 271–339.

33. Arnold Toynbee contends that not only will most learning be done informally, but that the professionalization of education may have reduced educational standards. "The essence of humane education has still to be acquired mainly through the informal apprenticeship that is the heart of education in all societies and all social classes at all levels. This is what makes and keeps us human. Book learning in 'the humanities' can be a valuable supplement to it, but can never be a substitute for it. . . . But the quality of education of all kinds depends on the quality of the people who give it, and there has been a paradoxical tendency for quality to

deteriorate as the formal element in education has increased in importance. The spontaneous apprenticeship in life, which was the only form of education known to early man, was given by the leaders of the community. . . . When a separate formal kind of education makes its appearance, it brings into existence a new class of professional teachers who work, like other professional men and women, for pay; and, in most societies in process of civilization thus far, both the pay and the status of the professional teacher have been lower than has been warranted by the lip service that society has paid to the value of formal education. This has sometimes set up a vicious circle, in which the depression and discontent of the teaching profession has deterred able people from entering it, and has thereby led to a further lowering of its standards and status." ("Education: The Long View," in *Saturday Review,* Nov. 19, 1960, pp. 78–80.)

34. For an excellent example of one who appreciates this integral relation between "education" and a total culture, see Gunnar Myrdal, *Asian Drama: An Inquiry Into the Poverty of Nations* (Random House, Inc., 1968), particularly Chs. 29, 31–33, in Vol. III.

35. In discussing *The Transmission of American Culture* (Harvard University Press, 1959), George Spindler contends that teachers "are agents of their culture. . . . They are not selected at random as official cultural transmitters; they are trained and accredited to that status and role" (p. 20).

36. Among anthropologists who view culture as an organism so that each feature of the culture is to be analyzed and understood as fulfilling a function within that organism are B. Malinowski, R. Firth, A. R. Radcliffe-Brown, and G. P. Murdock.

37. Ward H. Goodenough, in *Cooperation in Change* (John Wiley & Sons, Inc., 1963), expresses this distinction as "phenomenal" vs. "ideational." The first is the observed events in a community and the regularities they exhibit. The second is the organization of their experience by members of a community—a product of cognitive and instrumental learning. The phenomenal order is an artifact of the ideational order. See pp. 11 ff.

38. Jacques J. Maquet, writing about "Objectivity in Anthropology" in *Current Anthropology,* Vol. 5, No. 1 (February, 1964), comments about the rise of the field in relation to colonialism in the eighteenth and nineteenth centuries, when the "home country" needed help in understanding the "colonies," and he goes on to write that the anthropologist, "limited by his individual characteristics and his existential situation, will not pretend to offer

impersonal knowledge but will claim that his results are valid and perspectivistic. . . . It is to this approach that we owe nearly all our knowledge of man and society. . . . The unexpected consequences of the de-colonization process and the emergence of new states in Africa has been to lay bare, to some Africanists at least, the perspectivistic character of their discipline" (pp. 54 f.).

39. A number of anthropologists have been particularly interested in tracing evidences and examining the influences of cross-cultural contacts. Among them:

Barrett, H. B., *Innovation: The Basis of Social Change.* McGraw-Hill Book Company, 1953.
Mead, Margaret, *Cross Cultural Aspects of Technical Change.* Mentor Book. New American Library, Inc., 1955.
Van Nieuwenhuijze, C. A. O., *Cross-Cultural Studies.* The Hague: Mouton & Co., 1963.

40. The literature on the relation of anthropology to education is limited because only a few anthropologists have given particular attention to the subject, and also because some who have included considerations of education in their studies of a culture have had such an inadequate understanding of the field of education. Among the better books dealing with the relation between the two fields are:

Spindler, George D. (ed.), *Education and Anthropology.* Holt, Rinehart and Winston, Inc., 1955.
Brameld, Theodore, *Cultural Foundations of Education.* Harper & Row, Publishers, Inc., 1957.
Gruber, F. C. (ed.), *Anthropology and Education.* University of Pennsylvania Press, 1961.
Spindler, George D. (ed.), *Education and Culture: Anthropological Approaches.* Holt, Rinehart and Winston, Inc., 1963. This book includes extensive bibliographical material; see particularly pp. 79–83.

41. "Present generations are witnesses to the process of shrinking sociocultural world space, due to which the starting point for interrelations between the several parts of mankind is bound to be fundamentally revised. Thus far these interrelations have always had secondary status, whereas the way of life to which one belonged was the number one datum. By now the interrelations are due to achieve at least equal rank, if not primary importance. We cannot afford to omit shifting focus; we must reason, starting from mankind as a whole, toward component parts, or at any rate no

longer the other way round. Whether we like it or not, the accent has been shifted.

"A parallel shift is on the way as regards the manner in which theory deals with these matters. In developing the rationalizations that will be the tools of our intellectual approach to reality, we are bound to look for that which has a validity much more general than for our way of life only. Insofar as we succeed in establishing rationalizations that are adequate from this point of view, we can trust that we shall meet the demands actually being made upon ourselves as social scientists." (C. A. O. van Nieuwenhuijze, *Cross-Cultural Studies*, p. 127.)

42. James K. Feibleman, in *The Institutions of Society* (London: George Allen & Unwin, Ltd., 1956), defines an institution as follows: "An institution is an established social group working in customary ways with material tools in a common task. The institution, we might add, is the social function in a steady state. But the steady state does not preclude dynamism. To maintain a consistent flow of power, a more or less reliable structure is required. An institution organizes folkways and usually laws into a unit which serves a number of social functions." (P. 21.)

43. J. O. Hertzler, in *Social Institutions* (University of Nebraska Press, 1946), provides the following outline of the general functions of institutions:

Institutions satisfy basic individual and social needs in a cooperative way.

Institutions function as the operative bases of the social order.

Institutions are the major instruments of social control.

Institutions pattern the social behavior in the individual and in groups.

Institutions function as carriers of the society's culture.

Institutions function as social conservators.

44. Gordon Allport's *Institutional Behavior* (University of North Carolina Press, 1933) provides one of the few psychological analyses of many kinds of institutions: governmental, business, industrial, family, educational, and religious. For further reading on institutional characteristics and dynamics, see:

Blau, Peter M., and Scott, W. Richard, *Formal Organizations*. Chandler Publishing Company, 1962.

Etzioni, Amitai, *The Bureaucratic Phenomenon*. The University of Chicago Press, 1964.

March, James G., and Simon, Herbert A., *Organizations*. John Wiley & Sons, Inc., 1959.

45. However, the dangers of borrowing the images and institutional structures of other social agencies may be very great, as is illustrated by Fred M. Newmann and Donald W. Oliver as they write on "Education and Community" in *Harvard Educational Review*, Vol. XXXVII, No. 1 (Winter, 1967). "Education, having developed a concept of formal compulsory instruction publicly sponsored, could conceivably have taken many forms. . . . In the long run, however, education adopted the prevailing institutional structure in the society at large: the factory served by an industrial development laboratory and managed according to production-line and bureaucratic principles. Architecturally, the schools came to resemble factories (instruction carried on first in rooms but more recently in large loft-like spaces, with different spaces reserved for different types of instruction) and office buildings (with corridors designed to handle traffic between compartments of uniform size). Conceivably, schools could have been built like private homes, cathedrals, artists' studios, or country villas.

"The schools came to be administered like smooth-running production lines. Clear hierarchies of authority were established: student, parent, teacher, principal, superintendent, and school committeeman, each of whom was presumed to know his function and the limits of his authority. Consistent with the principle of the division of labor, activities were organized into special departments: teaching (with its many sub-divisions), administration, guidance, custodial services, etc. The process of instruction was seen by the administrator as a method of assembling and coordinating standardized units of production: classes of equal size, instructional periods of equal length; uniform 'adopted' books and materials that all students would absorb; standard lessons provided by teachers with standardized training. Departures or interruptions in the routine were (and still are) discouraged for their potentially disruptive effect on the overall process (e.g., taking a field trip, or showing a film that requires two periods' worth of time, or making special arrangements to meet with students individually). Conceivably, the schools could have been organized on a much less regimented basis, allowing a good deal of exploratory, random, unscheduled sort of activity. However, as Callahan (1962) persuasively argues, the corporate bureaucratic model, guided by the cult of efficiency, exerted a major influence on the organization and program of public education.

"In our view the effects of corporate organization in education lead to three major developments all of which have important contemporary implications: (*a*) the research and development mentality which limits its attention to finding and building technology and instrumentation to achieve given specifiable goals, rather than questioning or formulating the goals themselves; (b) the increasingly fragmented school environment, which is sliced according to administrative and subject matter categories prescribed by educational specialists rather than according to salient concerns of children, youth, or the larger community; and (c) the trend toward centralized, coordinated decision-making for schools by a combination of agencies in government, business, universities, foundations, and 'non-profit' research and development institutes." (Pp. 83 f.)

46. For the most comprehensive account of the development of the university in Europe, see the three volumes of Hastings Rashdall, *The Universities of Europe in the Middle Ages* (London: Oxford University Press, 1895, 1951).

47. Sylvia Ashton-Warner, working among Mauri children in New Zealand, was acutely aware of the cultural conflicts precipitated by British patterns she was expected to employ, so she created a different approach to childhood education that was relevant to the situation of the children she was serving. Her description of the children and of the methods she developed are presented in *Teacher* (Simon and Schuster, Inc., 1963).

48. Terry N. Clark writes of institutionalization as "the process whereby specific cultural elements or cultural objects are adopted by actors in a social system. It is thus a process basic to all social organizations, particularly formal organizations." ("Institutionalization of Innovation in Higher Education: Four Models," in *Administrative Science Quarterly*, Vol. XIII, No. 1, June, 1968, p. 1.)

49. Thorstein Veblen was particularly sensitive to this shift in institutional objectives, and credited the shift to "business" influences on university operations. He wrote: "It appears, then, that the intrusion of business principles (accountancy, standardization, piecework) in the universities goes to weaken and retard the pursuit of learning, and therefore to defeat the ends for which the university is maintained. This result follows, primarily, from the substitution of impersonal, mechanical relations, standards and tests, in the place of personal conference, guidance and association between teachers and students; as also from the imposition of a mechanically standardized routine upon the members of the staff, whereby any disinterested preoccupation with scholarly or scientific inquiry is thrown into the background and falls into abeyance. . . . The system of standardization and accountancy has (this) renown or prestige as its chief ulterior purpose—the prestige

of the university or of its president, which largely comes to the same net result." (*The Higher Learning in America: A Memorandum on the Conduct of Universities by Business Men* [1918; Reprint, Augustus M. Kelley, 1965], pp. 224, 227.)

50. In reviewing *Prelude to Riot: A View of Urban America from the Bottom,* by Paul Jacobs (Random House, Inc., 1967), Martin Duberman makes this summary of one of the explicit themes of the book: "Our urban institutions are, in their corruption, their racist assumptions, their disdain for the poor, an accurate mirror of the society that created and perpetuates them. Our institutional model is becoming paramilitary. The well-being of the organization takes precedence over the well-being of the people it was meant to serve. Order and efficiency become ends not means, and individual needs are irritably viewed as impediments to the smooth functioning of the system." (*The New York Times Book Review,* Jan. 21, 1968, p. 22.)

51. "A bureaucratic order approaches the stage of alienation in proportion as its 'unintended by-products' become a stronger factor than the original purpose. The heightening percentage of alienation corresponds with an intensification of class struggle because, at the point where the accumulation of unintended by-products is becoming impressive and oppressive, there will be a class of people who have a very real 'stake' in the retention of the ailing bureaucracy." (Kenneth Burke, "Bureaucratization of the Imagination," quoted in *Perspectives by Incongruity,* ed. by Stanley E. Hyman with the assistance of Barbara Karmiller (Indiana University Press, 1964), p. 77.

52. See Ira S. Steinberg, *Educational Myths and Realities* (Addison-Wesley Publishing Company, Inc., 1968), and his discussion of the mythology of democratic education.

53. Among recent books that provide valuable insights into the nature and problems of professionalism are:

Joffe, Ellis, *Party and Army: Professionalism and Political Control in the Chinese Officer Corps.* Harvard University Press, 1965.
McGlothlin, William J., *Patterns of Professional Education.* G. P. Putnam's Sons, 1960.
Reader, William J., *Professional Men: The Rise of the Professional Classes in 19th Century England.* Basic Books, Inc., 1966.
Vollmer, H. M., and Mills, Donald L. (eds.), *Professionalization.* Prentice-Hall, Inc., 1966.

Of particular interest is the article by Ernest Greenwood, "Attributes of a Profession," in Vollmer and Mills (eds.), *op. cit.* He asserts that "succinctly put, all professions seem to possess: (1) systematic theory, (2) authority, (3) community sanction, (4) ethical codes, and (5) a culture" (p. 10), and then proceeds to describe two aspects of professionalism that contribute to institutionalism. First is the assumption of authority: "Every profession strives to persuade the community to sanction its authority within certain spheres by conferring upon the profession a series of powers and privileges. Community approval of these powers may be either informal or formal. . . . Among its powers is the profession's control over its training centers. . . . The profession also acquires control over admission into the profession." (P. 13.) Secondly, asserts Greenwood, each profession develops a "culture" which he describes as follows: "To succeed in his chosen profession, the neophyte must make an effective adjustment to the professional culture. Mastery of the underlying body of theory and acquisition of the technical skills are in themselves insufficient guarantees of professional success. The recruit must also become familiar with and learn to weave his way through the labyrinth of the professional culture." (P. 18.)

54. Though there is a vast library of books about teaching and the teacher, N. L. Gage contends that scientific research during the past generation has focused upon learning to the virtual exclusion of research on teaching methods. So in an article in the *Phi Delta Kappa*, June, 1968 (pp. 601–606), he outlines the way such research might be conducted and describes some specific steps already taken by the Stanford (California) Center for Research and Development in Teaching.

55. Of course the same thing is true of the student who meets an educational occasion by his own imaginary projection of the teacher's (or school's) world. This is one of the reasons why a teacher is necessary, particularly in helping a student see what Bruner calls "the structure of subject matter." See Jerome S. Bruner, *The Process of Education* (Harvard University Press, 1962), particularly pp. 17–32.

Karl Mannheim, in *Ideology and Utopia: An Introduction to the Sociology of Knowledge* (Harcourt, Brace and World, Inc., 1966), illustrates this need in another context. "It can be shown in the case of Marxism that an observer whose view is bound up with a given social position will by himself never succeed in singling out the more general and theoretical aspects which are implicit in the concrete observations that he makes. It might have been expected, for instance, that long ago Marxism would have formulated in a more theoretical way the fundamental findings of the sociology of knowledge concerning the relationships between human thought and the conditions of existence *in general,* especially since its discovery of the theory of ideology also implied at least the beginnings of the sociology of knowledge. That this implication could never be brought out and theoretically elaborated, and at best only came partially into view, was due, however, to the fact that, in the concrete instance, this relationship was perceived only in the thought of the opponent. . . . Thus we see how the narrowed focus which a given position imposes and the driving impulses which govern its insights tend to obstruct the general and theoretical formulation of these views and to restrict the capacity for abstraction. There is a tendency to abide by the particular view that is immediately obtainable, and to prevent the question from being raised as to whether the fact that knowledge is bound up with existence is not inherent in the human thought-structure as such." (Pp. 248 f.)

56. Israel Scheffler amplifies on the claim that a student has upon a teacher when he writes: "To teach, in the standard sense, is at some points at least to submit oneself to the understanding and independent judgment of the pupil, to his demand for reasons, to his sense of what constitutes an adequate explanation. To teach someone that such and such is the case is not merely to try to get him to believe it: deception, for example, is not a method or a mode of teaching. Teaching involves further that, if we try to get the student to believe that such and such is the case, we try also to get him to believe it for reasons that, within the limits of his capacity to grasp, are *our* reasons. Teaching, in this way, requires us to reveal our reasons to the student and, by so doing, to submit them to his evaluation and criticism." (*The Language of Education,* p. 57; Charles C Thomas, Publisher, 1960. Quotations are used by permission of the publisher and the author.)

57. In a monograph *The Teacher and the Machine: Observations on the Impact of Educational Technology* (mimeographed, University of Chicago, 1966), P. W. Jackson described his view of what individualized instruction means. "Individualizing instruction, in the educator's sense, means injecting humor into a lesson when a student seems to need it, and quickly becoming serious when he is ready to settle down to work; it means thinking of examples that are uniquely relevant to the student's previous experience and offering them at just the right time; it means feeling concerned over whether or not a student is progressing, and communicating that concern in a way that will be helpful; it means offering appropriate praise, not just because positive reinforcers strengthen response tendencies, but because the student's performance is deserving of

human admiration; it means, in short, responding *as* an individual *to* an individual."

58. "Brainstorming, more or less as it is practiced today, was founded by him [Alex Osborn, an executive vice-president of Batten, Barton, Durstine and Osborn, in 1939] as a brilliant counterattack on negative conference thinking. . . . Brainstorming is a strategy with which a problem can be attacked—in fact, literally stormed, by dozens of ideas. The attack can be carried on by one person, by two or three, by an Osborn's dozen, or by even hundreds. The important thing is that the most creative portion of the brain, the subconscious, has its full fire directed right at the problem under attack. Ideas—new, different, crazy ideas—are allowed to get to the subconscious and set off the marvelous chain reaction of free association." (Charles H. Clark, *Brainstorming*, p. 53; Doubleday & Company, Inc., 1958.)

59. For a timely, though admittedly partisan, interpretation of the basis for "consenus" in the political arena, see William S. White, *The Professional: Lyndon B. Johnson* (Fawcett Publications, Inc., 1964), particularly pp. 76 ff. in the chapter "A Lady and an Art."

60. Two comments on Socrates' method help to illumine the significance of Socratic dialogue: "A dramatism of the mind sways Plato's works, and what appears as a dialectic of thought is at the same time the expression of an inward process in the thinker himself. But the point towards which and from which this living thought-process is set in motion, and this dramatism evolves, is Socrates. Plato's thought does not work from out of living in the manner of a monologue, but springs continually from the living tensions which arise between master and disciple, between the pioneer and his opponents—as, indeed, it was awakened in himself by that contact, made at the height of his youthful receptivity, which led to many years' fellowship of life and learning." (Romano Guardini, *The Death of Socrates: An Interpretation of the Platonic Dialogues*, p. vii; Sheed & Ward, Inc., 1948.)

W. Kenneth Richmond, in *Socrates and the Western World: An Essay in the Philosophy of Education* (London: Alvin Redman, Ltd., 1967), quotes W. W. Jaeger (*Paideia*, II, 36) who points out that "there was a profound symbolic resemblance between Socrates' conversations and the act of stripping to be examined by the doctor or trainer before entering the ring for a contest" (p. 150).

61. Richard S. Peters places considerable emphasis upon the place of "worthwhileness" in education. He writes: " 'Education'

does not imply, like 'reform,' that a man should be brought back from a state of turpitude into which he has lapsed; but it does have normative implications, if along a slightly different dimension. It implies that something worthwhile is being or has been intentionally transmitted in a morally acceptable manner. It would be a logical contradiction to say that a man had been educated but that he had in no way changed for the better, or that in educating his son a man was attempting nothing that was worthwhile. This is a purely conceptual point. Such a connection between 'education' and what is valuable does not imply any particular commitment to content. It is a further question what the particular standards are in virtue of which activities are thought to be of value and what grounds there might be for claiming that these are the correct ones. All that is implied is a commitment to what is thought valuable." (P. 25, *Ethics and Education*, by R. S. Peters. Copyright George Allen & Unwin, Ltd., 1966. Quotations are reprinted by permission of Scott, Foresman and Company.)

62. Religious educators are sometimes more tempted than others to express their goals completely in alumnal stage terms. One illustration is James D. Smart's "redefinition" of the goal of Christian education. He wrote: "Our goal must be no lesser goal than that which Jesus and the apostles had before them. We teach so that through our teaching God may work in the hearts of those whom we teach to make them disciples wholly committed to his gospel, with an understanding of it, and with a personal faith that will enable them to bear convincing witness to it in word and action in the midst of an unbelieving world. We teach so that through our teaching God may bring into being a Church whose glory will be the fullness with which God indwells it in his love and truth and power, and whose all-engrossing aim will be to serve Jesus Christ as an earthly body through which he may continue his redemption of the world. We teach young children and youths and adults that by the grace of God they may grow up into the full life and faith of his Church, and may find their life's fulfillment in being members of the very body of Christ and sharers in his mission." (*The Teaching Ministry of the Church*, p. 107; The Westminster Press, 1954.)

63. One might call this a "production model," the validity of which is effectively questioned by R. S. Peters in *Authority, Responsibility and Education* (London: George Allen & Unwin, Ltd., 1954). See pp. 84 f.

64. Jerome S. Bruner places greatest emphasis upon skills, and writes in *Toward a Theory of Instruction* (W. W. Norton & Com-

pany, Inc., 1966), "It would seem, from our consideration of man's evolution, that principal emphasis in education should be placed upon skills—skills in handling, in seeing and imaging, and in symbolic operations, particularly as these relate to the technologies that have made them so powerful in their human expression." (P. 34.)

65. Puerto Rico provides an especially interesting illustration of this view of the function of education. See Everett Reimer, "Technical Aspects of Educational Planning: A Case Study of Puerto Rico," in *Educational Planning and Socio-Economic Development in Latin America*, ed. by Joseph Fitzpatrick (Sondeo No. 9, Cuernavaca, Mexico, Center of Intercultural Documentation, 1965).

66. E. Paul Torrance reports that "Guilford and his associates at the University of Southern California have devised an interesting new way of classifying these thinking abilities. According to this model there are 120 mental abilities. Thus far, about fifty-six have been identified. Five mental operations are applied to three kinds of content and six kinds of products.

"A look at these mental operations is necessary in order to grasp something of the nature of the creative thinking abilities and the difference between these abilities and those sampled by traditional measures of intelligence. First, we have the cognitive operations, involved in recognizing, becoming aware of, and the like. Second, we have memory, which comes into play in retaining what has been cognized. Next, we have two kinds of productive thinking used in producing something new from what has been cognized and memorized. Divergent thinking is involved when possible solutions are many, whereas convergent thinking proceeds toward a restricted answer or solution. Finally, the evaluative abilities are involved when we assess what has been cognized, memorized, and produced, to determine its correctness, suitability, or adequacy." (*Education and the Creative Potential*, p. 93; University of Minnesota Press, 1963.)

67. Bruce Raup describes this view of the function of education in *Education and Organized Interests in America* (G. P. Putnam's Sons, 1936) with these words: "Education and the schools, whether they will or not, are involved instrumentally in the process whereby a civilization and a culture are continually remade. To teach a child is to modify in some way the social inheritance. The school selects first what shall be taught. It prefers some ideals, some beliefs to others. Then the child selects. The whole class selects, despite any appearance of conformity. When the bases

of a civilization and a culture are disrupted and confused, this selection becomes a definite contribution to a modified future." (P. 3.)

68. Frank G. Jennings, writing on "The New Dimension of Education" in *Saturday Review*, Feb. 13, 1960, observed: "Our society is undergoing a structural change so profound that no aspect of our lives will remain untouched by it. This change is reflected with particular force in the sharpened public perception of the functions of education. Margaret Mead recently indicated one element of it by redefining education to include 'another whole dimension of learning: the lateral transmission, to every sentient member of society, of what has just been discovered, invented, created, manufactured, or marketed.' By this she means to contrast the traditional role of education, which she calls 'vertical transmission of the tried and true by the old, mature, and experienced teacher to the young, immature, and inexperienced pupil in the classroom.'

"But far more than a shift in educational emphasis is involved. We are confronted with an emergent synthesis of demands which in fact is converting us into an educating society, forever teaching, learning, and sharing new understandings, new perceptions, and the achievement of new creative possibilities. Education has traditionally preceded life work, but today it is more and more becoming coextensive with it. And with this development new and generally unheralded allies of education have entered the lists.

"Today American business spends much more time, money, and energy on in-service education than we as a nation spend on our public and private schools." (P. 34.)

69. Israel Scheffler illustrates the difficulty in specifying the goals of education in his analysis of the use of the traditional term "growth." He wrote: "How shall we understand, to take but one example, the popular contention that growth is the goal of education? Clearly not every sort of growth is held desirable, witness growth in ignorance or brutality. Even if we eliminate obviously undesirable dispositions, shall we think of growth as simply the increase in dispositions acquired by the learner? This will not do, for a substantial part of growth consists in dropping off dispositions once mastered. We all at one time could shoot marbles pretty well but can do so no longer. Furthermore, in attempting a count of dispositions how shall we classify them? Is playing checkers one and playing chess another? If so, where do we put Chinese checkers? Finally, how shall we weight the progressive intensification of one disposition as against the multiplication of several?

"Taking a new direction, we might, along lines reminiscent of Dewey, consider growth as the intensification of some master disposition, e.g., the ability to solve problems intelligently. But how is such intensification itself to be construed concretely? A simple increase in solved problems per unit of time may not indicate growth if conjoined with a greater increase per unit of time in perceived problems remaining unsolved. Shall we propose, then, as an appropriate indication of our meaning here, the ratio of solved problems to those perceived, per unit of time? This would end in absurdity since, other things remaining equal, a decrease in perception would constitute growth, while an increase in sensitivity to problems would constitute regression. We might try a different move (as Dewey appears to in certain of his writings), and construe problems not as relative to the selectivity of a perceiver, but as somehow objectively built into the total situation. But such a move, while it is not obvious that it meets our original difficulties, clearly raises more troubles than we had to begin with: just what is a total situation, what kind of entities are objective problems, and how do we determine their character?" ("Toward an Analytic Philosophy of Education," in *Harvard Educational Review*, Vol. XXIV, Fall, 1954, pp. 223–229.)

70. A particularly explicit formulation of national commitment as the alumnal goal of education was voiced by Hollis L. Caswell, then president of Teachers College at Columbia University, as reported in *The New York Times*, Feb. 10, 1960. "Dr. Caswell said that he was convinced the educator of today had to understand education's goals and purposes as well as the learning process and then 'relate these to the community's needs.'

"A school's objectives are determined by 'the goals of our country,' he noted, and the teacher needs a firm grounding in basic American values to determine what values the community is seeking. 'Then the teacher can try and foster these values in this curriculum,' he said."

71. C. F. Melchert (in a manuscript entitled "An Exploration in the Presuppositions of Objective Formation for Contemporary Protestant Christian Educational Ministry," scheduled to be published by Yale University Press in 1969) provides a valuable analytical evaluation of the concepts of goals for education of R. S. Peters, Marc Belth, and Jerome Bruner. While he struggles with the attempt to find a "core" of education (what Belth calls the "root") and speaks of objective in the singular rather than recognizing that the goal is always a set of objectives related to the various semiautonomous processes of education, he still makes a valiant

attempt to identify the basis of educational autonomy. "Thus the educational process, in its autonomy, has a characteristic intentionality about it, which does not seek justification for its existence by reference to some end beyond itself. The function of that which is called objective is found within the process, in clarifying that intentionality, and not outside the process explaining it. Thus it is not an educational question to ask what is the purpose of education. It is an educational question to ask what is the purpose of some activity within the educational process." (Pp. 105 f.)

72. A particularly helpful examination of the many ethical dimensions of education is to be found in R. S. Peters' book, *Ethics and Education*.

73. R. S. Peters includes this type of encounter within his concept of education as initiation. He writes, " 'Initiation' is a peculiarly apt description of this essential feature of education which consists in experienced persons turning the eyes of others outwards to what is essentially independent of persons." Initiation also describes the other aspect of education that "those who are being educated should want to do or master the worthwhile things which are handed on to them." ("Education as Initiation," in *Philosophical Analysis and Education*, ed. by Reginald D. Archambault, p. 106; Humanities Press, Inc., 1965.)

74. Michael Polanyi offers a valuable insight into the inseparability of the subjective and the objective within a person committed to the truth, in *Personal Knowledge: Toward a Post-Critical Philosphy* (The University of Chicago Press, 1958), in a section titled "The Subjective, the Personal and the Universal" (pp. 300 ff.).

75. Jerome Bruner suggests that the study of learning has been limited too much to the objective, to techniques, to factors that can be analyzed in laboratories, "the realm of the right hand," while insufficient attention has been given to sentiment, intuition, and art, "the realm of the left hand." Bruner explores the relation between the two in *On Knowing, Essays for the Left Hand* (Harvard University Press, 1963), because he is convinced that "the artificial separation of the two modes of knowing cripples the contemporary intellectual as an effective mythmaker for his times" (pp. 2 f.).

76. Getzels and Jackson conducted an interesting study of creativity among high school students in terms of the relation of I.Q. to creativity. They make clear a distinction between academic achievement and creativity, and include a strong indictment of teachers who prefer the former to the latter. "It is possible to begin by identifying two basic cognitive or intellective modes. The one

mode tends toward retaining the known, learning the predetermined, and conserving what is. The second mode tends toward revising the known, exploring the undetermined, and constructing what might be. A person for whom the first mode or process is primary tends toward the *usual and expected*. A person for whom the second mode is primary tends toward the *novel and speculative*. The one favors certainty, the other risk. Both processes are found in all persons, but in varying proportions.

"Various terms have been used to describe the two processes. Guilford has suggested 'convergent thinking' and 'divergent thinking'; Rogers uses 'defensiveness' and 'openness'; Maslow 'safety' and 'growth.' Whatever terms are used, it is clear that one process represents intellectual acquisitiveness and conformity, the other, intellectual inventiveness and innovation. One focuses on knowing what is already discovered, the other focuses on discovering what is yet to be known." (Pp. 13 f.)

"The data are quite clear-cut. The high IQ group stands out as being more desirable (to teachers) than the average student, the high creativity group does not. . . . Even though the scholastic performance is the same, the high IQ students are preferred over the average students by their teachers, the creativity students are not. The result is quite striking for, if anything, the reverse should be true. Here is a student—the high IQ one—who is doing scholastically only what can be expected of him. Here is another student—the high creativity one—who is doing scholastically *better* than can be expected of him. Yet it is the former rather than the latter who is enjoyed more than the average student by his teachers." (Pp. 30 f.)

"The essence of the performance of the high creativity adolescents lay in their ability to produce new forms, to risk conjoining elements that are customarily thought of as independent and dissimilar, to 'go off in new directions.'" (P. 52.) (Jacob W. Getzels and Philip W. Jackson, *Creativity and Intelligence: Explorations with Gifted Students;* John Wiley & Sons, Inc., 1962.)

Rollo May, the existentialist psychiatrist, provides a somewhat different approach to "The Nature of Creativity" in *Creativity and Its Cultivation*, ed. by Harold H. Anderson (Harper & Brothers, 1959). May is concerned to counteract "the oversimplification and inadequacy of the depth-psychological theories of creativity" (p. 55). One of these is the "*compensatory theory of creativity*. This is, briefly, that human beings produce art, science, and other aspects of culture to compensate for their own inadequacies. . . . The theory does have some real merit and is partially true. But its error is that it does not deal with the *creative process as such*" (p. 56). "The other most widely current psychoanalytic theories about creativity have two characteristics. First, they are *reductive*. That is, they reduce creativity to some other process. Secondly, they generally specifically make it an expression of *neurotic* patterns. The usual definition of creativity in psychoanalytic circles is 'regression in the service of the ego.'" (P. 56.)

May disagrees with these theories. He presents a much more positive interpretation, defining creativity "as the process of *bringing something new into birth*. . . . Creativity is the most basic manifestation of man's fulfilling his own being in his world" (p. 57). Although he illustrates his theory primarily in the field of art, May is careful to indicate the parallel nature of creativity in other fields. His theory is based upon two observations, first that the creative act "is an encounter" (p. 58). "The essential point is not the presence or absence of voluntaristic effort, but the degree of absorption, the degree of intensity; there must be a specific quality of *engagement*." (P. 59.) This encounter must be with reality, not an escape from reality.

77. In *The Concept of Mind* (London: Hutchinson's University Library, 1949), Gilbert Ryle precipitated a continuing dialogue among educators by suggesting that the basic distinction of types of learning is between learning *that* and learning *to*.

78. Or as Ward H. Goodenough expressed it, "We stimulate shifts in the perception of our fellows by inviting them to consider themselves in the light of other considerations" (*Cooperation in Change*, p. 221).

79. "Innovative leaders have frequently been marginal men; a large number of innovations seem to come from quasi-outsiders, persons occupying statuses in two or more institutional realms. One reason for their greater innovativeness is that marginality leads to exposure to activities in more than one sphere, which makes innovation possible by applying ideas and procedures from one sphere to a second." (Terry N. Clark, "Institutionalization of Innovation in Higher Education," in *Administrative Science Quarterly*, Vol. XIII, No. 1, June, 1968, p. 15.)

80. "Everybody needs a glimpse of the bird's-eye view, with a radius of hundreds of miles, that one catches from a jet plane flying in the stratosphere. Everybody also needs to have a glimpse of the worm's-eye view, with the depth of thousands of feet, that one catches by sifting the successive strata that are brought to the surface by an oil prospector's drill as it burrows into the bowels of the earth. The capacity of a single human mind is nar-

rowly circumscribed; it can never succeed either in surveying the whole surface of the globe or in probing the globe's interior to the center. Yet at least it need not confine itself to either of these intellectual quests exclusively. It can sample both, and such intellectual catholicity will be a liberal education." (Arnold J. Toynbee, "Education: The Long View," in *Saturday Review*, Nov. 19, 1960, p. 81.)

81. Obviously, relating imagination to perspective does not exhaust the relation of imagination to educational processes. Imagination is a fascinating subject for study in itself, and one's understanding of the nature and functions of imagination in cognitive and creative acts would directly influence any relation to educational processes. The following are two complementary descriptions of the functions of imagination.

"It may be said that the *primary* work of the imagination is to 'objectify' objects; to arrest the blind rush of phenomena by amalgamating their contents with the forms of the mind. . . . Through this indissoluble combination pure imagination forms the logical base for all acts of knowledge, as it gives to understanding a 'stable' referent. . . . The intention of such a theory of imagination is to explain the 'synthesis of understanding,' not to afford cognitive content to the 'synthesis of understanding,' or even to an 'imagination of reason.' Rather, on this view, pure imagination is made to serve a function of mediating synthesis; to insure the applicability of categories to experience; to insure that concepts will not be empty and percepts blind. . . . The transcendental imagination mediates order, structure, and regularity to nature." (Roy L. Hart, "The Role of Imagination in Man's Knowledge of God," Ph.D. thesis, p. 212; Yale University, 1959.)

"We may conclude that any theory of imagination must satisfy two requirements. It must account for the spontaneous discrimination made by the mind between its images and its perceptions. And it must explain the role that images play in the operations of thought. Whatever form it took, the classical conception of images was unable to fulfill these two essential functions. To endow an image with a sensory content is to make it a thing obeying the laws of things, not the laws of consciousness. The mind is thus deprived of all hope of distinguishing images from the other things belonging in the world. By the same token, there is no way at all to conceive the relation of this thing to thought. Indeed, by removing images from consciousness, we deprive the latter of all its freedom, and by introducing images into consciousness, the whole universe follows after, solidifying consciousness at one stroke, like a supersaturated solution." (Jean-Paul Sartre, *Imagination,* pp. 117 f.; University of Michigan Press, 1962.)

Among significant books exploring the uses of imagination in the arts, sciences, and religion are the following:

Collingwood, R. G., *The Historical Imagination.* London: Clarendon Press, 1935.

Kroner, Richard, *The Religious Function of Imagination.* Yale University Press, 1941.

McKeller, Peter, *Imagination and Thinking.* London: Cohen & West, Limited, Publishers, 1957.

Willey, Basil, *Coleridge on Imagination and Fancy.* London: Geoffrey Cumberledge, 1947.

82. Émile Durkheim once observed that "it is possible to explain only by making comparisons"; quoted in Godfrey Lienhardt, *Social Anthropology* (London: Oxford University Press, 1964), p. 37, which may reflect one reason for the preoccupation with comparative studies of cultures at one stage in the development of the field of anthropology.

83. Four studies that illustrate variety in the use of "perspective" are:

Lee, Sir Sidney, *The Perspective of Biography.* London: Oxford University Press, 1918.

Saurat, Denis, *Perspectives.* Paris: Stock, 1938.

Walsh, Warren B., *Perspectives and Patterns: Discourses on History.* Syracuse University Press, 1962.

Waterman, J. T., *Perspectives in Linguistics.* The University of Chicago Press, 1963.

84. Philip H. Phenix has suggested that the traditional disciplines should be regrouped together in the following six "realms of meaning":

Symbolics: Ordinary Language, Mathematics, Nondiscursive Symbolic Forms.

Empirics: Physical Science, Biology, Psychology, Social Science.

Esthetics: Music, the Visual Arts, the Arts of Movement, Literature.

Synnoetics: Personal Knowledge.

Ethics: Moral Knowledge.

Synoptics: History, Religion, Philosophy.

See *Realms of Meaning: A Philosophy of Curriculum for General Education* (McGraw-Hill Book Company, Inc., 1964).

85. R. S. Peters indicates a fine appreciation of the motivation of some educators who were committed to the growth concept of education when he writes: "The suggestion is not that, as a matter of historical fact, growth theorists pondered on the concept of 'education' and mistakenly puffed up some minimal conceptual intimations into a procedural principle. More probably their concept of education was moulded by their consciences; for they were morally indignant at the lack of respect shown for children as individuals and appalled by the lack of psychological understanding evident in the ways in which they were treated. Their moral indignation and increasing psychological insight were combined in procedural principles demanding that children should be treated with respect, not indoctrinated, coerced or ordered around, and that they should be allowed to learn by experience and choose for themselves." (*Ethics and Education*, p. 42.)

86. There is often confusion about the relation of "theory" to "philosophy" in education. O'Connor provides a helpful analysis of the various senses in which the term "theory" is employed: "It will be useful to distinguish the main senses of the word (theory). (1) Sometimes the word is used, as in philosophy, to mean no more than 'a body of related problems.' It is in this sense that philosophers talk of 'the theory of knowledge' or 'the theory of value.' (2) It may also be used to refer to a very highly organized and unified conceptual framework with little or no relation to any practical activity. For example, mathematicians talk of 'the theory of numbers' or of 'group theory.' (3) When in ordinary speech we contrast theory with practice we refer to a set or system of rules or a collection of precepts which guide or control actions of various kinds. . . . Educational theory would then consist of those parts of psychology concerned with perception, learning, concept formation, motivation and so on which directly concern the work of the teacher. In this vague sense of the word, then, 'theory' means a general conceptual background to some field of practical activity. And such a conceptual background is usually in some degree unified and systematic so that parts of the theory are logically related to other parts. This degree of system will naturally be highest in a highly developed science like physics. (4) There is however a more technical sense of the word 'theory' which it is useful to consider here because it is a sense that gives us standards by which we can assess the value and use of any claimant to the title of 'theory.' In particular, this sense of the word will enable us to judge the value of the various (and often conflicting) theories that are put forward by writers on education. The model or paradigm of

theories in this, the most important, sense of the word is to be found in natural science and particularly in the more developed sciences like physics or astronomy. Even in these restricted fields, the word 'theory' has no one perfectly definite meaning. But it is most often used to refer (a) to a hypothesis that has been verified by observation and, more commonly, (b) to a logically interconnected set of such hypotheses." (D. J. O'Connor, *An Introduction to the Philosophy of Education*, pp. 75 f.; London: Routledge & Kegan Paul, Ltd., 1957.)

87. The relation of philosophy to educational practice continues to disturb those who attempt to develop a philosophy of education. A direct examination of the problem has been attempted by a group of British writers under the editorship of Reginald D. Archambault, in *Philosophical Analysis and Education*. Of particular interest is the initial paper by L. Arnaud Reid, "Philosophy and the Theory and Practice of Education." Reid suggests, first, that educational theory is a "social phenomenon" which "comes into being through the conversation together of different experts who have the care for education as a common concern" (p. 21). He contends that philosophy which analyzes only is inadequate for education. " 'A philosophy of education' will be a more worked out, systematic treatment of those aspects of educational theory which are susceptible to philosophical treatment." (Pp. 26 f.) Reid attacks the idea that educational practice can be deduced from general philosophical positions, such as idealism, realism, or empiricism, because "practical policy is not just a logical deduction (though it may contain some passages of deduction) but an educational *judgment*, a principled decision, made in the light of all the relevant factors in the individual educational situation" (p. 29). A philosophy of education is practical, he says, in that it helps the educator "act with more insight and intelligence" (p. 33).

88. Peters elevates the "responsibility of the teacher" in a moving passage in *Ethics and Education*. After pointing out that for many centuries the role of the teacher was traditional and circumscribed, he says: "Nowadays all this is changed. There are no set systems of teaching and no agreed aims of education; there is constant controversy about the curriculum and a welter of disagreements about how children ought to be treated. In more settled times only the very reflective teacher was led to probe behind tradition for a rationale of what he ought to do, nowadays it is only the lazy or the dogmatic teacher who can avoid such probing. Neither can the modern teacher find in the appeal to authority much more than a temporary resting place; for authorities disagree, and on

what grounds is the advice of one rather than another to be heeded? The unpalatable truth is that the modern teacher has no alternative to thinking out these matters for himself." (P. 93.)

89. Many books on "philosophy of education" employ this deductive procedure—exploring the implications of various recognizable philosophical positions for the field of education. One of the more adequate publications of this type is *Modern Philosophies and Education,* ed. by Nelson B. Henry (National Society for the Study of Education, The University of Chicago Press, 1955), a symposium of papers that trace the educational implications of ten philosophical positions.

90. Arthur Guiterman wrote,

> "For Education is, Making Men;
> So it is now, so was it when
> Mark Hopkins sat on one end of a log,
> And James Garfield sat on the other."

(From "Education," in *The Light Guitar,* p. 20; Harper & Brothers, 1923.)

91. The popular images of education are often expressed in slogans which, says Scheffler, "provide rallying symbols of the key ideas and attitudes of educational movements. They both express and foster community of spirit, attracting new adherents and providing reassurance and strength to veterans. They are thus analogous to religious and political slogans and, like these, products of the party spirit" (*The Language of Education,* p. 36).

92. It was Alexander Pope, in his *Moral Essays,* who affirmed that

> " 'Tis education forms the common mind;
> Just as the twig is bent the tree's inclined."

(From *The Poetical Works of Alexander Pope,* Vol. II, Epistle I, line 149; Edinburgh: James Nichol, 1866.)

93. "Aqueducts and canals may serve to irrigate some far country, *but not the country through which they pass.* So formal rational, rectilinear education may serve to pass the water on to some future time and place, but it does little or nothing in the moment. For true education is not like the aqueduct or the canal, which carries water rationally or in a prescribed manner to a predetermined destination; rather it is like the river which seeks out the secret nature of the terrain through which it flows and always respects it! Because it respects it, it may transform it; indeed the terrain will never be the same after the river flows through it, percisely be-

cause the river seeks it out and meanders through all its crevices and depressions. Or, the river may rush torrentially down its mountainside, advancing rapidly and relentlessly. But this it can only do because it seeks out the easiest passage, the most evident place to tumble majestically into the valley. Then too, neither the mountain, nor the valley, nor (indeed!) the river will ever be the same—because the river has respected the terrain and sought out its inevitable logic.

"All of this is directly parallel to true education.

"The way the wind relentlessly and affectionately seeks out the inner, permanent pattern of a rock, or a tree, or a mountain, is only another way of saying the same thing." (Ricardo Arden Couch, unpublished, used by permission.)

94. George H. Williams, in a monograph prepared for the tricentennial of Harvard University, *The Theological Idea of a University* (National Council of Churches, 1958), traces the development of the image, from the medieval period to the present, of the university as a paradise, a fresh Garden of Eden, symbolized even in the campus as a garden. Later he expanded this theme into a book, *Wilderness and Paradise in Christian Thought: The Biblical Experience of the Desert in the History of Christianity, and the Paradise Theme in the Theological Idea of the University* (Harper & Row, Publishers, Inc., 1962).

95. "The educator deals consciously with the common culture. He not only transmits but helps remake it." (Bruce Raup, *Education and Organized Interests in America*, p. 5; or see George Counts's book, *Dare the School Build a New Social Order?* The John Day Company, 1932.)

96. See note 45.

97. "True believer" is a term popularized by Eric Hoffer in his book *The True Believer* (Harper & Brothers, 1951), a quasi-sociological analysis of the need of some individuals to have all decisions made for them, and of societies to have many "followers" if leaders are to be able to accomplish their objectives.

98. See note 34.

99. Israel Scheffler has provided a helpful distinction in the types of definitions of education that are common currency. In *The Language of Education* he identifies the stipulative, descriptive, and programmatic definitions. "A general definition is often simply a stipulation to the effect that a given term is to be understood in a special way for the space of some discourse or throughout several discourses of a certain type. Such a definition may be called 'stipulative.' A stipulative definition exhibits some term to be defined and

gives notice that it is to be taken as equivalent to some other exhibited term or description, within a particular context. It is a piece of terminological legislation that does not purport to reflect the previously accepted usage of the defined term—if indeed there is such a predefinitional usage at all. Stipulative definitions may in turn be divided into two groups, depending on whether, in fact, the defined term has such a prior usage to begin with. Where it does not, the stipulative definition may be called an 'inventive' stipulation. Where, on the other hand, the stipulative definition legislates a new use for a term with a prior, accepted usage, it may be called a 'non-inventive' stipulation." (P. 13.)

"Once it is established that a stipulative definition or set of such definitions is formally coherent and pragmatically well-chosen, it is irrelevant to argue against it further on the ground that it fails to reflect the normal meaning of the defined term or terms. *In this special sense*, stipulative definitions may be said to be matters of arbitrary choice." (P. 15.)

"It is evident that descriptive definitions [to provide explanatory accounts of meaning] are not matters of arbitrary choice in the way in which stipulative definitions have been said to be. For beyond formal and pragmatic considerations, descriptive definitions may be called to account in respect of the accuracy with which they reflect normal predefinitional usage." (P. 16.)

Scheffler indicates that definitions of education also have a practical or programmatic role. "It is through this practical role that general definitions are often keyed fairly directly into social practices and habits of mind. . . . Roughly speaking, some terms . . . single out things toward which social practice is oriented in a certain way. . . . To propose a definition that now assigns such a term to some new thing may in context be a way of conveying that this new thing ought to be accorded the sort of practical treatment given to things hitherto referred to by the term in question. . . . Similarly, to propose a definition that withholds such a term from an object to which it has hitherto applied may be a way of conveying that the object in question ought no longer to be treated as the things referred to by the given term have been treated.

"Even if a definition is proposed that assigns the term just exactly to the objects to which it has hitherto applied and to no others, the point at stake may be to defend the propriety of the current practical orientation to such objects and to no others, rather than (or as well as) to mirror predefinitional usage.

"Where a definition purports to do either of these three things, it is acting as an expression of a practical program and we shall call it 'programmatic.' . . .

"Thus it is the practical purport of the definition *on a particular occasion* that reveals its programmatic character." (Pp. 18 f.)

Scheffler notes that "the same definitional equation may be stipulative, descriptive or programmatic, depending on the context in which it is offered" (p. 20), but each has an underlying interest: "The interest of stipulative definitions is communicatory, that is to say, they are offered in the hope of facilitating discourse; the interest of descriptive definitions is explanatory, that is, they purport to clarify the normal application of terms; the interest of programmatic definitions is moral, that is, they are intended to embody programs of action" (p. 22).

100. See Jonas F. Soltis, *An Introduction to the Analysis of Educational Concepts*, pp. 2 f.

101. Consciousness is essential to education and this is expressed in the use of language. R. S. Peters, in *Ethics and Education*, relates consciousness and language to the "public world" into which education introduces a person. "The point is that consciousness, which is the hall-mark of mind, is related in its different modes to objects. The individual wants *something*, is afraid or angry with *somebody* or *something*, believes or knows that *certain things are the case*. The objects of consciousness are first and foremost objects in a public world that are marked out and differentiated by a public language into which the individual is initiated. The learning of language and the discovery of a public world of objects in space and time proceed together. But the individual, as owner of experiences welded to each other in a unique life-history, represents a particular and unrepeatable viewpoint on this public world." (P. 50.) "Education consists essentially in the initiation of others into a public world picked out by the language and concepts of a people and in encouraging others to join in exploring realms marked out by differentiated forms of awareness." (P. 52.)

102. As indicated in the Introduction, education frequently is viewed as normative in a moralistic sense, as an activity whereby society produces a particular type of behavior. We have attempted to show that this is an inadequate view. However, R. S. Peters contends that educational processes in themselves have a normative dimension in another sense, that is, that it is an activity which always "implies that something worthwhile is being or has been intentionally transmitted in a morally acceptable manner." See full quotation in note 61.